# MISSING LINKS
## The Challenges to Further Education

*Informing policy by establishing objective facts*

The Policy Studies Institute (PSI) is Britain's leading independent research organisation undertaking studies of economic, industrial and social policy, and the workings of political institutions.

PSI is a registered charity, run on a non-profit basis, and is not associated with any political party, pressure group or commercial interest.

PSI attaches great importance to covering a wide range of subject areas with its multi-disciplinary approach. The Institute's 40+ researchers are organised in teams which currently cover the following programmes:

*Family Finances and Social Security*
*Health Studies and Social Care*
*Innovation and New Technology*
*Quality of Life and the Environment*
*Social Justice and Social Order*
*Employment Studies*
*Arts and the Cultural Industries*
*Information Policy*
*Education*

This publication arises from the Education programme and is one of over 30 publications made available by the Institute each year.

*Information about the work of PSI, and a catalogue of available books can be obtained from:*

Marketing Department, PSI
100 Park Village East, London NW1 3SR

# MISSING LINKS
## The Challenges to Further Education

**Stuart Maclure**

PSI
PUBLISHING

**PUBLISHING**

The publishing imprint of the independent
POLICY STUDIES INSTITUTE
100 Park Village East, London NW1 3SR
Telephone: 071-387 2171; Fax: 071-388 0914

ISBN 0 85374 511 0

A CIP catalogue record of this book is available from the British Library.

**1 2 3 4 5 6 7 8 9**

**How to obtain PSI publications**
All book shop and individual orders should be sent to PSI's distributors:

BEBC Ltd
9 Albion Close, Parkstone, Poole, Dorset, BH12 2LL

Books will normally be despatched in 24 hours. Cheques should be made payable to BEBC Ltd.

Credit card and telephone/fax orders may be placed on the following freephone numbers:

FREEPHONE: 0800 262260 FREEFAX: 0800 262266

**Booktrade Representation (UK & Eire)**
Book Representation Ltd
P O Box 17, Canvey Island, Essex SS8 8HZ

**PSI Subscriptions**
PSI Publications are available on subscription.
Further information from PSI's subscription agent:

Carfax Publishing Company Ltd
Abingdon Science Park, P O Box 25, Abingdon OX10 3UE

Laserset by Policy Studies Institute
Printed in Great Britain by Billing and Sons Ltd, Worcester

# Acknowledgements

I should first acknowledge my indebtedness to the Policy Studies Institute for the invitation to spend a year at the PSI as a Distinguished Visiting Fellow from September 1989 to August 1990. The Institute is a stimulating place and like others who have experienced its warm but invigorating climate I have a lot to thank its chairman, Sir Richard O'Brien and director, Bill Daniel, for. The Distinguished Visiting Fellowships at PSI are funded by the Joseph Rowntree Foundation to whom my thanks also go.

I owe a lot, too, to the members of a seminar which met at intervals through the first half of 1990 to discuss the future of further education. In no sense is this book a representation of the views expressed – nobody is to blame for what follows but me – but I benefited greatly from the comments of those to whom sections of it were circulated in draft, among them G.M. Austin, Christopher Ball, David Bradshaw, Richard Bird, Clive Brain, John Cassels, Roger Crowther, Malcolm Fraser, Anne Jones, John Lorriman, Richard O'Brien, Graham Philips, John Sellars, Hilary Steedman; special thanks, too, to Geoffrey Melling and the Further Education Staff College from whom I received much help and phrases which may have crept into the text unacknowledged; to Geoff Stanton, Gilbert Jessup, Eric Bolton, SCI, and David Sharp, HMI; to Ian Johnston, John Cridland and Richard Gorringe; and to John Baillie, Jenny Shackleton and John Temple who contributed the material which appears on pages 58 to 69, and also made comments at various stages; and to Amanda Trafford who organised the seminars and helped to organise the manuscript.

**Stuart Maclure**
February 1991

# Contents

# 1  Points of Departure

> Further Education is not just the bit in between school and higher
> education. It is not just the Cinderella of the education service...
> Over 1,750,000 attend further education classes... taught by the
> equivalent of 63,000 lecturers. There are some 400 LEA-
> maintained colleges. The whole thing costs over £1 billion a year
> It is a big, big enterprise.[1]

This was the Rt.Hon Kenneth Baker MP, the then Secretary of
State for Education and Science, addressing the Association of
Colleges for Further and Higher Education (ACFHE), in February,
1989. He was speaking as the architect of the Education Reform Act,
passed the previous year, and he was seeking to carry the argument
forward:

> We have set in hand the changes which will achieve a better
> foundation at age 16. Now I believe that the time is ripe to give a
> similar powerful thrust towards education and training thereafter
> – building on the work already done through TVEI. In short, it is
> time for an initiative to promote Further Education.

When Kenneth Baker spoke these words, he raised expectations
which have not so far been realised. What he said was right. The time
has come when a clear and forward-looking policy for further
education should be set out and pursued with boldness and vigour.
Only by clarifying aims and strategy can the full, under-used and
under-valued resources – human and physical – of further education
be put to most effective use.

Three recent developments underline the importance of a new deal
for further education: the Education Reform Act; Government
projections for higher education; and the CBI Report *Towards a Skills
Revolution*.

## The **Education Reform Act, 1988**

This, the most far-reaching piece of educational legislation since 1944, was mainly concerned with the education of pupils in school.[2] It introduced a national curriculum from 5 to 16 along with various measures to create more choice and competition. It strengthened the hands of parents as consumers. It removed the polytechnics and colleges of higher education from local authority control and set up new funding arrangements for them and for the universities. It also clarified the legal basis for further education and reorganised the finance and governance of the colleges.

The national curriculum will affect the FE colleges in due course if it raises the standards of attainment among school-leavers and provides the hoped for 'better foundation' on which to build opportunities post-16.

Stronger governing bodies and more financial delegation will increase the colleges' ability to respond to new demands – and, in particular, demands for an expansion of vocational education and training.

The main impact of the Act on further education, however, has been indirect and paradoxical. By focusing strongly on the compulsory school period 5-16, it has thrown into relief the egregious deficiencies of the education system beyond 16 – the high drop-out rate, the poor record in vocational education and industrial training, and the contrast between the higher education participation rate in Britain and in other advanced countries. None of these topics was addressed in the Act.

What the Act did was to highlight the unfinished business of educational reform – the tasks which need to be tackled with the same commitment and zeal which ministers have devoted to the national curriculum and the crusade for parent power. The Act showed that a bold government could intervene directly in areas (like, for example, the school curriculum) where it had been commonly assumed it must stand off.

With his well-developed political antennae, Kenneth Baker was quick to recognise these wider implications; his ACFHE speech was an attempt to ride the wave and use it to build up the momentum needed to mobilise support among 'the colleagues' for the shake-up of vocational education and industrial training which everyone knows is long overdue.

**Government projections for Higher Education**

A few weeks before his speech on further education, Kenneth Baker had hit the headlines with an address at Lancaster University (in January 1989) in which he speculated on the growth of higher education over the next twenty-five years.[3] He noted that numbers had more than doubled in the quarter of a century before 1989 and believed that 'there is scope over the next 25 years for even greater advance'. By the end of the 1990s he expected the participation rate among 18 year-olds to have risen from about 15 per cent to 'something approaching 20 per cent' and went on to discuss a scenario for 'mass higher education' with a doubling of the participation rate within the 25-year time-span.

It was a carefully-worded speech – not about government plans for achieving an expansion of higher education but about the sociological consequences of economic development. He believed that greater wealth would foster higher expectations as in North America. And as the number of graduates in the population steadily increased, they would insist on more higher education for their children.

There were many implications for further education in the Lancaster speech. It brought out clearly that expansion would also have to mean diversification and that much of that would relate to vocational education. It implied a broader definition of higher education – the admiring references to American practice raised in the minds of some people the American equation of higher with post-secondary.

It was also obvious that the opportunity for 18 year-olds was only likely to increase in the proportions which Baker envisaged if there was a steady increase in the participation rate from 16-18. Clearly there would also be more adults making their way back into mainstream education (with all that this would imply for FE). And clearly, too, an expanded higher education network would include more part-time and distance learning: it would not be simply more of the same. But even so, it was inherently unlikely that the top of the pyramid could be indefinitely raised without also retaining more students within the education system beyond 16, many of them on a full-time basis. The same sociological and economic trends on which the Secretary of State relied for his prediction on higher education, therefore, point to a corresponding rise in demand for further education among the 16 to 18s and among older students.

**Towards a Skills Revolution: The report of the CBI Task Force**[4]
In the autumn of 1989, the Confederation of British Industry (CBI)
adopted a radical report on vocational education and training prepared
by a Task Force of senior industrialists. Without equivocation, this
declared that 'the practice of employing 16-18 year-olds without
training leading to nationally recognised qualifications must stop'.

Paragraphs 21-23 speak of a 'revolution' in the delivery and
finance of vocational education and training:

> Foundation skills are the foremost priority. The transition from
> education to work has been the weakest element of Britain's skills
> provision and this has made the updating of adult competence both
> difficult and expensive...

> The Task Force believes that there is no longer any good case for
> under-18 employment which is not at the same time raising skill
> levels. By 1992 all 16 and 17 year-olds should be undertaking
> education and training relevant to their needs. The Task Force
> proposes that any under-18 employment not involving structured
> education and training leading to recognised qualifications should
> be eliminated...

> The Task Force believes that it is necessary to set world class
> targets for the progress which should be made during the period of
> foundation learning by young people from age 16-19 to secure a
> more highly skilled workforce for the future and satisfy individual
> aspirations...

The CBI targets were expressed in terms of National Vocational
Qualifications (NVQs) – using the terminology and categories
developed by the National Council for Vocational Qualifications. By
1995 'almost all' young people should attain NVQ level II or its
academic equivalent and all young people should be given an
entitlement to structured training, work experience and education
leading to NVQ level III. By 2000, 'half the age group should attain
NVQ level III or its academic equivalent'.

And alongside these foundation provisions, the CBI proposed
ambitious targets for the training and retraining of adults – by 1995,
at least half the workforce should be working for updated
qualifications within the NVQ framework; and by 2000, 50 per cent
of the employed workforce should hold NVQ level III or equivalent.

Implicit in the Task Group's analysis is the belief that Britain is
not just under-trained but under-educated *and* under-trained. The same
conviction imbues *Britain's Real Skill Shortage*[5] by John Cassels –

the real shortage is of competence at all levels including the managerial and professional. What the CBI calls a 'skills revolution' is in reality something which goes much deeper than a simple training deficit.

'Skills' is a word that enjoys a current popularity because it sounds functional and practical. But vogue words need to be pinned down. In his ACFHE speech, Kenneth Baker offered his gloss on it: 'By "skill" I mean competence, built on knowledge and understanding. Attainment of skills in this wider sense is not just the capacity to perform a particular task, nor is it the empty acquisition of factual knowledge. It is the coming together of competence, knowledge and understanding...'. In this sense, the CBI's concerns spread right across the spectrum which links the most academic of education with the most specific of training.

It should be noted that the rationale adopted by the Task Group is economic throughout: 'to maintain and improve Britain's position in an increasingly competitive world nothing short of a skills revolution is required'. The long and inconclusive arguments about the economic return on investment in education are set aside: it is simply assumed that the vicious circle of low skills, low wage, low profit, low productivity, outlined by Finegold and Soskice in their celebrated article in the *Oxford Review of Economic Policy* (Vol 4, No 3, 1988), has to be broken and that this implies a massive investment in human capital. The same assumptions underpin John Cassels' analysis.

As the Institute of Public Policy Research paper[6] on *A British Baccalaureat* (of which David Finegold was a joint author) points out, this has now become part of the conventional wisdom, which a Conservative Secretary of State for Employment and the Labour Party's policy document on industry find equally easy to accept. The Task Force drew the common sense conclusion that there is a link between the education and training policies of rich countries (and those which are rapidly becoming rich) and their commercial success. They did not confine their references to Europe, North America and Japan: no foreign example was more telling than that of South Korea which is said to be 'aiming by the end of the century for 80 per cent of its young people to reach university entrance standard'. (It is not necessary to assume that the CBI knows much about university entrance standards in South Korea to recognise that the South Koreans mean business.)

It is interesting to speculate on why British industry should have suddenly seen the light. Anybody who has followed these matters

5

It is interesting to speculate on why British industry should have suddenly seen the light. Anybody who has followed these matters over a period of years has heard the arguments many times before and waits for the scoffing replies from sophisticated critics, as well as from the exponents of what Correlli Barnett calls 'the cult of the Practical Man'.[7]

'How relevant are foreign examples?' a voice would say. 'You cannot reproduce the experiences and social pressures of Japan, South Korea or the Federal Republic of Germany, in England. If you could, would you want to?'

It is extraordinary how many ways there are of expressing old fashioned national complacency – 'We've heard all this so many times before but the fact is we do things differently here – we have our ways, they have theirs. At their best our ways serve us well. There is something in the English character which is resistant to formal education and training. There is no way, for instance, that the compulsory general education included in the curriculum of the German Berufsschule could be foisted on English teenagers...' And there is no argument which cannot be made more complicated by taking it to pieces – 'Why are you so sure that it is education and training which account for the superiority of economic performance abroad? What about management? unions? supervisory staff? the banking system? Don't we need a lot more information before embarking on expensive and precarious cultural revolutions?'

To their credit the CBI have cut through the argument and put their money on education and training without getting bogged down in argument about theory. The underlying economics remain debatable. Not all investment in education and training earns the same rate of return but the CBI have made the conclusive judgment that there is a 'significant and widening skills gap' which demands a 'quantum leap in skill levels throughout the workforce'.

## A history of failure
Why it should have seemed obvious to so many for so long that the English need less – or are capable of absorbing less – education and training than other nations is not clear. Nor is it obvious why they have leant so easily to the view that prosperity was best served by concentrating on high standards for a narrow elite.

What is indisputable, however, is the strength of the individual and institutional resistance which has thwarted one attempt after another to reform vocational education and training over many decades – a cultural phenomenon which goes back at least as far as the abortive attempts to reform technical and vocational education in the last quarter of the nineteenth century.

Anybody interested in 'a powerful thrust towards education and training' now, must have this weight of past experience in mind.

It is more than 70 years since parliament first enacted provisions which, like the CBI proposals, would have kept all young people within the framework of education and training up to the age of 18. The Day Continuation sections of the 1918 Act required compulsory full-time attendance at school up to 14, and for those who then left, compulsory attendance for eight hours a week (320 hours a year) at Day Continuation classes between the ages of 14 and 18. The Lewis Committee, whose work foreshadowed these clauses in the 1918 Act, sought

> ...nothing less than a complete change of temper and outlook on the part of the people of this country as to what they mean, through the forces of industry and society, to make of their boys and girls. Can the age of adolescence be brought out of the purview of economic exploitation and into that of the social conscience? Can the conception of the juvenile as primarily a little wage-earner be replaced by the conception of the juvenile as primarily the workman and citizen in training?[8]

The idealism of the CBI Task Force was cloaked in the language of national, corporate and individual interest but it, too, seemed to pin its faith on a spontaneous cultural revolution which would change the mind-set of the nation. Universal structured education and training to 18 could be achieved, the Task Force believed, but it depended on a big 'if'. All would be plain sailing

> ...if young people, educationalists, Government, unions and employers come together to make it happen.

Day Continuation Schools of the 1918 Act succumbed to the slump in the 1920s and became a dead letter. The 1944 Education Act made another attempt. It raised the minimum school leaving age by stages from 14 to 16 and provided for County Colleges which school leavers would have to attend, part-time, to 18. The German model was much in people's minds and the proposed extension of day release assumed a reform of apprenticeship and industrial training which never happened. So county colleges joined day continuation schools among the might-have beens and some forty years later, the lapsed clauses of the 1944 Education Act were repealed in the Education Reform Act of 1988.[9]

It is a matter of history how one half-hearted attempt after another to do something about industrial training and vocational education came to nothing during the 1950s and 1960s.

I cannot be alone in recalling hours spent at conferences organised by bodies like the British Iron and Steel Trades Federation in the early 1950s, listening to reports from the 'productivity teams' sent (with Marshall Aid) to study what happened in America. The travellers returned to preach the gospel of training and vocational education. The shortcomings of rigid apprenticeships were carefully dissected. The importance of top-management commitment to staff development and training was duly rehearsed. Then everyone went away, to meet again six, twelve, eighteen, months later, to chew over yet again the iniquity of rigid age limits on apprenticeships, the poverty of operative training, the lack of technicians, the lack of interest and involvement on the part of top management.

Step by step, over the years, successive British Governments found themselves backing gingerly into the active role they tried so hard to avoid. The Industrial Training Councils failed to deliver; to be replaced after the passing of the Industrial Training Act of 1964 by the Industrial Training Boards, levying and granting their way to their own decline; and on to the Employment and Training Act of 1973 and the arrival of the Manpower Services Commission, forerunner of the short-lived Training Agency, now incorporated in the Department of Employment.

Looked at in perspective, it is a remarkable and deeply shameful story of the persistent failure of government, industry and education to grasp basic national needs. Throughout the 1950s and 1960s, governments felt absolved of any responsibility because it was accepted doctrine on all sides that training was a matter for the employers and unions – a by-product of industrial relations. It was not till the 1970s, when the rise of unemployment (and especially youth unemployment) created the political necessity for governments to be seen to act, that the dogged sloth so sedulously cultivated by the Ministry of Labour, gave way to the frenetic activity of the MSC. And as soon as the immediate threat of youth unemployment began to subside, ministers saw less need for national policies to remedy past failures and slipped back into the familiar rhetoric which left training to the market place.

## Cultural legacies

The failure to tackle industrial training in the thirty years which followed the end of the Second World War had a profoundly damaging effect on education as well as training. Had there been a thriving training scene, the demand for vocational education and vocational preparation would have been stimulated and authenticated.

In the absence of stronger links with industry, at the intermediate and lower levels as well as at the professional level, there was little chance of creating a real alternative ladder via vocational education, as for example, the Crowther Committee had hoped in 1959.[10]

Sir Christopher Ball is only the latest observer to point to the cultural factors which influence attitudes to education and training and help to explain peculiar English deficiencies.[11] Such writers as Martin Wiener[12] and Corelli Barnett have explored the debilitating aspects of English life over the past century and a half which have coalesced to form the set of class attitudes which have made the upper classes despise wealth creation and led other large sections of the population to conclude that extended education was not for them.

It has been easy enough to find scapegoats. Industry's training failures have been roundly condemned by critics inside and outside the ranks of the industrialists. Education has been criticised as one of the means by which an anti-industrial culture has been handed down and made respectable. Education, in particular, has demonstrated the negative side-effects of the elitism which has been characteristic of the culture. Governments have been open to attack for failing to maintain consistent and effective policies, and inside the government machine there has been much damaging antagonism between the Department of Employment and the Department of Education.

Little is to be gained by analysis which seeks to fix the blame for these deep-seated cultural characteristics on any single set of institutions. It is of the nature of cultural traits that they reflect a wide range of interlocking social, economic and political phenomena – interlocking and interdependent as chicken and egg.

The educators have been blamed for imbuing generations of students with negative attitudes towards industrial employment. There is some truth in this accusation: but education reflects and transmits the values which are dominant in society and the values which have dominated English life for more than a century have not been those of the enterprise culture.

There is no way in which educational institutions can stand outside the society of which they are a part. Breaking into the circle depends on changing the dominant values, and even then it takes time for new assumptions to assert themselves. When, as now, there is a confusion of voices, the educators are bombarded with conflicting messages, the loudest of which say: do as I say, not as I do.

The MORI poll, conducted for the London Docklands Development Corporation in 1990[13] brought out clearly the social and cultural links which encourage (or inhibit) extended participation in education and training. One of the questions asked of a sample of boys and girls approaching the school-leaving age, concerned their attitude to staying on. Some 67 per cent said they wanted to stay on. But this rose to 85 per cent in the case of boys and girls who 'knew someone who had been through higher education' and fell to 53 per cent for those who had no such 'role model'.

If the culture of the universities, polytechnics, further education colleges and schools is to change in the ways needed to produce a 'world-class' workforce, educated and trained to the levels needed for the twenty-first century, it will be essential for the right messages to be passed down the line from the labour market.

If educators in general – and students in particular – are to get the message that industry values education and training and qualifications, it is essential that this should be the signal which employers send out in their recruitment and reward policies. The educational institutions certainly preach the importance of qualifications: they need all the extrinsic support they can get to motivate their students. In fact, they probably overstate the case and lead young people to expect their qualifications will be more highly valued than will be the case.

This was confirmed by the already quoted MORI poll. Many docklands employers said they paid little regard to educational qualifications of the young people they recruited and provided no training themselves. Whereas 66 per cent of the young people questioned said they thought qualifications were among the most important factors in getting a job, only 25 per cent of employers rated qualifications as important.

Persuading employers to value education and training is the critical task which faces the CBI in bringing about the cultural revolution to which it is committed. The colleges cannot 'sell' vocational education if employers contradict them by their example. It remains true today that the demand for, and vigour of, vocational education depends on employers giving practical backing in their personnel policies to the impeccable sentiments of the senior industrialists who set the pace in the CBI.

There is no prospect at the present time of legislation to force young workers to college or to force employers to train them though occasional voices argue that such legislation should be enacted.[14] But it is within the power of central and local government and other public sector employers to give a lead. If all public employers were as good as the National Health Service in this regard, there would be a significant increase in training.

An early date should be set by which all public sector employers should be required by the government to 'sign up' as corporate supporters of the CBI proposals. Without waiting for anybody else, they should adjust their recruitment and personnel policies accordingly and make quality training with day release a first priority for all their young employees.

### Targets: 'Foundations skills ... the foremost priority'

When *Towards a Skills Revolution* first appeared it was welcomed by ministers and Norman Fowler, the Secretary of State for Employment, endorsed the targets. Unfortunately this took place at the end of November 1989, shortly before he decided to spend more time with his family. His successor, Michael Howard, hastened to withdraw any implied government commitment. The government welcomed the report and noted the targets which the CBI had set up but made it clear they were not targets to which the government intended to be answerable.

Once again, there is tension at the centre of the debate about education and training between the clear need for a strong national policy and the official doctrine that vocational training is nobody's business but industry's.

Targets are needed in order to dramatise the drive to change industrial and educational practice. Without a legislative framework – some would say, without placing legal obligations on employers and young workers – there can be no hard and fast timetable for the achievement of specific training standards. But in the absence of legislation it is all the more necessary to adopt national working targets, which can then be used as yardsticks by which to measure voluntary progress. If it transpires that aims which have been agreed between the government and industry, and have been publicly endorsed as the nation's collective intentions, are not attained by exhortation alone, then there can be an informed debate about other forms of executive and legislative action. The virtue of national targets, nationally endorsed, is that they commit the government, as well as the CBI, to the skills revolution.

As it happens, the CBI targets have been effectively adopted by the Trades Union Congress[15] and the Labour Party's policy document *Investing in Britain's Future* sets out objectives which are consistent with those of the CBI. There is no reason to suppose that the Conservative Government has any quarrel with the CBI package – its welcome is quite genuine – but for ideological reasons it feels obliged to make it clear that the ball is in industry's court; and for immediate economic reasons it is reluctant to do anything which might imply any increase in public expenditure. The ideological inhibitions are misplaced; the financial scruples should be swiftly overcome and the government should come out now with a forthright endorsement of bold targets. Without such a commitment it is difficult to believe the CBI proposals can succeed.

What of the CBI targets themselves? How realistic are they? At times the CBI proposals read like yet another triumph of hope over experience. They may represent the best set of targets now on offer but it is difficult to justify the numbers by reference to any worked-out model of how they are to be achieved. They seem to have been plucked out of the air in desperation. The desperation may be justified, and the need for publicly-stated goals may be accepted, but not without a good deal of scepticism about the specific targets which have emerged.

More important than the targets for particular levels, measured in terms of 'NVQs and their academic equivalents', is the basic proposition that nobody should be in employment under 18 who is not in some form of structured education and training leading to recognised qualifications. This has certainly been endorsed by ministers but with no indication as to how this is to be achieved. The target numbers and percentages can be taken as illustrative of what this might mean rather than as a plan of action.

The attempt, in any rigorous way, to equate academic qualifications – GCSE and A levels – with those falling within the prospective ambit of the National Council for Vocational Qualifications is conceptually flawed. The use of the phrase 'academic equivalent' will become misleading unless serious thought is given to the relationship between the examinations which come within the purview of the School Examinations and Assessment Council and those which look to NCVQ.

There is no indication of how the CBI thinks the relevant population will divide between those who meet the CBI targets by achieving 'academic equivalents' and those who do so with NVQs.

The use of five GCSEs at grades A-C as a yardstick is yet another reminder that folk memories of the School Certificate and London matric die hard. It represents a standard which excludes more than two-thirds of those who now attend maintained secondary schools. Most of those who obtain five good GCSEs will remain within the education system to 18 and many of them will go on to higher education.

For the purpose of setting bold targets – which are essential – rough and ready equivalencies are acceptable: but if the influence of NCVQ were to extend over the territories where academic and vocational examining bodies overlap, it would be important to look more seriously at the underlying points of difference and similarity. It would be much more sensible to look for equivalencies in terms of National Curriculum Assessments – and the Levels 6-7 which most school students are expected to attain after eleven years of compulsory schooling.

## Implications for FE

According to the Education Statistics for the United Kingdom (1989 edition) more than half the 16-18 year-olds 'participated in post-compulsory education in 1987-88...; 18 per cent were in school, 33 per cent in further education (largely part-time, 20 per cent) and 4 per cent in higher education'. The part-time figures include YTS trainees. Twenty-eight per cent of 19 and 20 year-olds were continuing their education divided evenly between further education (mainly part-time) and higher education (mainly full-time).

The figures for 17 year-olds provide the most useful break-down in the present context:

| *In full-time education* | *percentage of age group*[1] |
|---|---|
| School | 19 |
| FE[2] | 13 |
| In employment outside YTS | 36 |
| On YTS | 21 |
| Unemployed | 10 |
| Of which in part-time day education (included in employed/unemployed)[3] | 7 |

Notes

(1) The figures are for Great Britain, January 1988, for students age as at 31 August of the preceding year.

(2) Excludes those on YTS within colleges.

(3) Public sector part-time day study only, excluding those attending YTS courses. The majority of part-time day students are in employment but some are receiving unemployment benefit under the '21 hour rule'.

(Source: *Education Statistics for the UK*, 1989 edition, Table 21)

A prime objective must be to create the circumstances in which the proportion of full-time students aged 17 can increase to the kind of levels which are found in other developed countries such as those quoted in DES Statistical Bulletin 1/90 – *International Statistical Comparisons of the Education and Training of 16 to 18 year olds*:

| | *percentage of the age group* |
|---|---|
| Australia | 50 |
| Belgium | 77 |
| Canada | 77 |
| Denmark | 68 |
| France | 68 |
| Germany | 43 |
| Italy | 47 |
| Japan | 89 |
| Netherlands | 77 |
| Spain | 52 |
| Sweden | 85 |
| United Kingdom | 34 |
| United States | 87 |

Note: Figures are for 1986 except for Germany (1987), Italy (1982), Japan (1988) Sweden (1985). The Bulletin also quotes a UK figure for 1988 of 35 per cent which differs from that in the already-quoted *Education Statistics for the UK*,1989.

This would imply at least a 50 per cent increase in the participation rate for full-time students, spread between schools and further education. This must be regarded as a very modest expansion if the same sociological factors which are expected to increase participation in higher education also affect behaviour among younger age groups.

It should be an object of policy to encourage this to happen. Ministers at the DES have welcomed the signs of a rising trend in staying on and made it clear that it is the government's wish that this should continue. In this regard, as in the matter of the higher education participation rate, they regard this as a cultural matter rather than as a matter on which positive policy is required. (The Labour Party policy document *Investing in Britain's Future* is more explicit, promising an Education Standards Council, one of whose tasks would be to agree targets for increased participation at 16 plus with each local education authority, which would then be monitored and revised from year to year.)

Labour also makes a cautious reference to 'easing the financial burden which prevents young people from low income groups from continuing with their education'. But given the financial constraints, Labour has moved away from earlier plans for more extensive educational maintenance allowances (EMAs). A sidelight on this is offered by the Dockland Survey to which reference has already been made. Among the young people in the sample, money was not the main reason stated for not continuing in education beyond 16 – more said they were leaving because they disliked school or had had enough of it – but one in five mentioned financial reasons. On average they said they would need £3,000 a year to stay on.

A fifty per cent expansion would mean that one in two 17 year-olds would remain in full-time education. This would still leave Britain near the bottom of the range among competitor nations along with Germany. It would certainly not be enough to match the levels expected among developing countries on the Pacific rim nor yet to take account of continuing development in Europe.

The comparison with Germany appears to be the most relevant if the CBI proposals for the expansion of part-time vocational education and training are pursued vigorously. But it has to be recognised that the comparatively low full-time participation rate in Germany is underpinned by a highly organised system of compulsory day release, and a network of specialised schools in which general and vocational education is provided according to agreed curricula. Such a well-established system carries the confidence of employers and of public opinion generally, with a well-defined role for the State and for trade unions as well as for the employers' organisations.

Critics have been quick to notice the ambivalence of government policy towards the German model. For some years it seemed that the German example was in the ascendant. The initiatives of the Manpower Services Commission in the Youth Opportunity Programme and in the two-year Youth Training Scheme were seen as a first step towards a national system for the induction of young people into employment with organised education and training for all. The influential report commissioned by the National Economic Development Office, *Competence and Competition,*[16] drew on experience in Japan, the United States and Germany and it, too, while insisting that all foreign experience must be understood in context, showed clear admiration for the German tradition.

More recently, however, the tendency has been to look to the United States for ideas and models. As an editorial in the University of Warwick's 'VET Forum' put it:

> Many American vocational education and training experts are surprised and confused to learn that Britain has been looking to their country for policy ideas. Surprised because they tend to view the British VET system as relatively successful, as evidenced by their recent interest in British initiatives like YTS, TVEI, and the National Curriculum; confused because the US education and training system is widely held to be in a state of crisis that no nation would want to emulate. Among its most serious problems are: significantly lower levels of attainment in basic subjects such as reading, maths and science than its main international competitors, high drop-out rates from secondary schooling, particularly in the inner cities, and growing skill shortages in key industrial sectors.[17]

A recent report by a study team based at the Massachusetts Institute of Technology, *Made in America,* makes the same point at considerably greater length, comparing American education and training unfavourably with Germany and Japan and applying to American industry, many of the criticisms now being levelled against British practice.[18]

The Warwick comment referred more directly to the setting up of Training and Enterprise Councils and the role of Cay Stratton, the American consultant brought in by the Department of Employment to share the experience she had gained working with Private Industry

Councils in Massachusetts. But it is relevant to the CBI proposals, too.

Britain has made several abortive attempts in the past to move in the German direction. It seems a reasonable conclusion that, in the British context, it makes more sense to try once more to make a success of this approach, than to reconstruct the secondary education system in such a way as to locate skill training inside educational institutions (as, for instance, in France or the US). In this respect, then, Britain is not going to adopt a North American model: but North American influences may well be strong enough to make sure that the German model is not followed with the degree of discipline on the part of employers which is necessary for success.

Present strategies assume that further education will continue to increase its share of the market for full-time students post-16 as well as expanding provision for those who attend part-time. Exactly how the full-timers will divide between schools and FE can only be a matter for speculation: the overlap in the provision of a variety of courses at GCSE and A level make this depend in large measure on the private choices of individuals. It is obvious that the schools' sixth form curriculum has to be reformed to take account of the National Curriculum from 5 to 16 and to provide the broader base which (among many others) the CBI Task Force demanded.

Many people doubt if there can be any serious attempt to rationalise provision for the 16-18 age range till this is confronted. But the politics of any such confrontation are extremely difficult because of the relationship between the traditional sixth form and the elite system of higher education which it serves. For the Conservatives, there is an obvious tension between the new conservative radicalism which sees traditional academe as the enemy of enterprise, and the old conservatism which is constrained to defend to the last A levels as essential guarantors of academic standards. It is easier in theory for Labour to take bold decisions on these matters. In *Looking to the Future*, another Labour policy document, there is a commitment to reform A levels on the lines advocated by the Higginson Committee, whose report was rejected out of hand by the Conservative Government when it appeared in 1988. But in office in the 1970s, Labour proved extremely cautious about examination reform because it was acutely sensitive to any accusation that it was 'soft on standards'.

It may be argued that the schools have their hands full with the curriculum reforms which are now in hand and could not cope with

17

yet another large-scale upheaval. There is much truth in this but the reappraisal of A levels cannot be unduly delayed; it is as urgently needed for further education as for the schools.

Without any deliberate national policy decision, the FE share of full-time education post-16 has been steadily growing, partly as a result of the spread of tertiary colleges, partly because more students have chosen to continue their studies in this way. The expectation must be that this trend will continue and that a growing proportion of those who remain in full-time education beyond 16 are enrolled in vocational courses such as those validated by the Business and Technician Education Council.

Assuming, then, a 50 per cent rise in the participation rate for 17 year-olds over the next ten years, coupled with progress in the expansion in structured part-time education and training for young workers for which the CBI is calling – the pattern might look something like this:

| *In full-time education* | *percentage of 17 year-olds* |
|---|---|
| School | 25 |
| FE | 25 |
| In part-time FE | |
| (including those in regular | |
| employment and the latter-day | |
| equivalents of YTS) | 25-30 |

This would leave in the year 2000 a residue of 25 per cent comprising those who are receiving structured education and training otherwise than at a FE college, and those who are employed by companies which have not accepted the CBI principles. Experience abroad suggests that there is a hard core of about 10 per cent for whom special arrangements would have to be made.

If the leaders of the CBI have their way, progress would be more rapid, and before the end of the century the bulk of the 16-18s not in full-time education would be accounted for in part-time FE or in structured programmes organised by employers themselves, or through private sector training organisations.

A great deal will depend on the economic climate. Demographic trends suggest that juvenile employment will be buoyant and wages will rise. This will raise the financial incentives for young people to drop out of full-time education. But it does not necessarily follow that more will do so: it could be that as in the later 1980s, the knowledge that employment prospects are good will give more young people the confidence to postpone entry into the labour market.

Most of the uncertainties which attend any target-setting for participation rates and FE numbers relate to considerations which lie beyond the concern or control of the educators. There are, however, two lines of policy which have been developing in recent years which hold the key to the new deal for further education which is now required. The first of these concerns curriculum and qualifications; the second, the changes in organisation, presentation and philosophy required to make the colleges responsive to contemporary needs. It is to the first of these that we now turn.

## Notes

1. Rt Hon Kenneth Baker MP, Secretary of State for Education and Science, *Further Education: A New Strategy*, Address to the Annual Meeting of the Association of Colleges for Further and Higher Education, 15 February 1989, DES 1989.
2. For a guide to the Education Reform Act, see Stuart Maclure, *Education Re-formed*, Hodder and Stoughton, London, second edition 1990.
3. Rt Hon Kenneth Baker MP, *Higher Education: the Next 25 Years*, Address given at Lancaster University, 5 January 1989, DES 1989.
4. *Towards a Skills Revolution*, report of a Task Force set up by the Confederation of British Industry, London 1989.
5. Sir John Cassels, *Britain's Real Skill Shortage*, Policy Studies Institute, London, 1990.
6. *A British Baccalaureat – Ending the Division between Education and Training*, Institute for Public Policy Research, London, 1990.
7. Correlli Barnett, *The Audit of War: Illusion and Reality of Britain as a Great Nation*, Macmillan, London, 1984.
8. Report of the Departmental Committee on Juvenile Education in Relation to Employment after the War (the Lewis Report), 1917. See Stuart Maclure (editor), *Educational Documents, England and Wales 1816 to the Present Day*, Routledge, Chapman and Hall, London, Fifth edition, 1986.
9. Education Reform Act, 1988, Section 120.
10. Report of the Minister of Education's Central Advisory Committee entitled *15 to 18* (the Crowther Report), 1959.

11. Sir Christopher Ball, *More Means Different: Widening Access to Higher Education*, Industry Matters, RSA, London, 1990.
12. Martin Wiener, *English Culture and the Decline of the Industrial Spirit, 1850-1980*, CUP, 1981.
13. MORI report on Attitudes of Young People and Employers towards Education in Docklands – research conducted for the London Docklands Development Corporation, 1990.
14. Richard Layard and Sig Prais, 'Time to think about compulsion', *Financial Times*, 15 March 1990.
15. Trades Union Congress, *Skills 2000*, 1989.
16. Institute of Manpower Studies, *Competence and Competition*, National Economic Development Office, 1984.
17. University of Warwick VET Forum Spring 1990, American Education Reform – in Britain?.
18. Michael L. Dertouzos, Richard K. Lester and Robert M. Solow, *Made in America – Regaining the Productive Edge*, The MIT Commission on Industrial Productivity, MIT Press.

# 2   Missing Links

If, then, we accept the CBI priority and look first at what the Task Group called the 'foundation' stage, how would we reorganise the provision now made for the education of the 14-18 age-groups if we were to decide as a matter of policy that everybody should remain in education and/or training on a full or part-time basis to the age of 18?

The question is posed in this way because it would not be enough to concentrate simply on the 16 to 18 age-range: the key change must be to persuade young people and their parents to stop thinking of 16 as the age when ordinary people complete their education. Instead, as the CBI has recognised, the programme from 14 to 18 must be organised as a continuum which embraces both full and part-time education for everyone.

This means that we cannot confine the discussion to further education or vocational education. We are concerned with the whole spectrum of education for the four age-groups who make up the three million or so 14-18 year-olds.

We are forced to return to the long-established weakness of the English education system – the fact that vocational education has never been properly integrated into the larger entity of secondary education. This means confronting the yawning gap between high-status 'academic' education and low-status 'vocational'; a gap which helps to disenfranchise half the secondary school population.

Towards the end of the 1980s the proportion staying on full-time tipped over the 50 per cent mark for the first time. The aim must be to maintain the positive trend till the social pressures which have in the past worked to induce a majority to leave are reversed and start to encourage staying on. Nothing less than this will do if we want a 'world-class workforce' which is both better educated and better trained.

This means that alongside the policy for training, there has to be an education-based strategy – one founded on a belief that educational institutions can be reformed and strengthened to take their full part. It means building on an already discernible recovery of nerve on the part of the Department of Education and Science. And given the world as it is, and the way power is distributed within the machinery of government, it means persuading the Department of Employment that it is better to try to strengthen the educational institutions than by-pass them.

To some this will appear to be yet another piece of special pleading on behalf of an education system which has been under severe attack. A lot of work in recent years has gone into building up, and giving recognition to, the learning which goes on in work. The Department of Employment, through the Training Agency, and the MSC before it, has placed great reliance on the work of Managing Agents (with or without the participation of FE colleges).

There are those who see any argument for enhancing the importance of FE as a throw-back to the heretical belief that learning can only take place within an educational institution – a claim for an unacceptable monopoly.

Not so. While it is wholly right to protect and build on the experience which has been gained from all the work of the Manpower Services Commission and the Training Agency, it is equally important not to let this deflect us from the task of overhauling the education system as it affects the 14-18s and getting it right. The tension between the education and training traditions – and their champions within government and elsewhere – is real enough. It cannot be ducked. But when all this is said and done, we should still decide as a matter of policy to capitalise on the huge unrealised potential of the FE colleges and exploit their capacity to respond to new demands.

It is this capacity to adapt and respond which should now occupy the centre of attention. Private sector training providers have an important role to play but there is no reason to accept defeatist arguments that the colleges are so set in their ways that they cannot accept the challenge. What must now be created is a robust, clearly-understood, *system* of education and training, backed by efficient, clear-sighted, open and strong but flexible institutions, which will provide a sturdy framework within which the needs of all 14-18 year-olds can be met.

The ultimate object must be a system which can carry large numbers forward without question and without agonising – a system which everyone takes for granted as part of the natural order of things.

## Present arrangements

At present the way forward is clear for those who are going on to A levels in schools or in FE – clear, that is if they get the necessary GCSEs at grades A to C to be accepted into their chosen A level courses. The route is relatively straightforward, too, for those (with four good GCSEs) who choose to transfer to BTEC national courses in FE.

These are the students who take the high road. It is not without its pitfalls – sometimes a third of those who take A levels fail – but it is a well-defined and relatively well-understood path and one which leads on to higher education for many who embark upon it.

For the rest, the way forward is much less clearly marked. Some stay on, in schools and in FE, to repeat subjects at GCSE; some embark on courses for the Certificate of Pre-vocational Education. Others can take college-based vocational courses for qualifications such as those of the Royal Society of Arts. The 'new' sixth form has grown over the past 20 years, moving from one expedient to the next, waiting for the promised reform of the sixth form curriculum and A levels, which has receded into an ever more uncertain future. For the 15 year-old, faced with a confusing and apparently haphazard catalogue of options, too much depends on individual initiative and know-how. The premium on knowing your way about the system – or non-system – is too high. It is as if the object was to put off the timid or doubtful – to make life difficult for the first generation stayer-on.

Nearly half the 16 year-olds do not choose any of these options but seek employment, with or without any guarantee of training. Some will join well-organised company training schemes and pursue recognised apprenticeships. Others will get little or no training. DES statistics estimate that four-fifths of all those who enter employment or YTS get some sort of education and/or training.[1] To reach this statistical conclusion it is necessary to adopt the broadest definition of what constitutes training.

If, as has been suggested, the same sociological factors which point to a steady increase in demand for higher education also foreshadow a near-equivalent increase in the proportion of 17 year olds who will expect to remain within full-time education, the options at 16 plus must be made a great deal clearer and simpler. This is equally true for those who take the part-time route as for those who take the high road. It is true that there are those who have a low opinion of schools and colleges and believe the employment-based route is much to be preferred. They would be suspicious of anything which might carry a hint of empire-building. But whether they are right or the exponents of more formal education are right, the choice will be made by 'the market' – the student-consumers who have the whip hand in a voluntary system. How they exercise their right to choose will depend on the evolution of English society over the next twenty years. All other developed countries have come to expect that their young people will spend longer periods in initial education and training – notwithstanding more adult education and retraining also. The likelihood must be that Britain will come to share this perception. The very least we can do is to create a framework which can accommodate a similar development here.

### Wanted: a robust framework

What we must do now, without waiting for the reform of A levels, is to think hard about the range of options which we want to hold out to young people as they approach the end of the compulsory school period. We have to be able to provide them with a clear map, outlining various routes forward. These routes need to be linked at many points, to ensure the maximum flexibility. As many as possible should be capable of leading on to higher and professional education, but the framework should not be dominated by those with high academic gifts. It should provide as clearly for those aiming to get qualifications of immediate relevance to employment.

A start should be made now by surveying what is already available in sixth forms and in FE colleges for full-time and part-time students.

A grid should then be put over the spread of activities, arranging them in broad categories. This would produce a limited number of programme areas within which work could be organised, learning modules produced, and students could exercise choice. Some of the mapping is already there in the framework which BTEC uses, but it would have to be extended to cover other vocational qualifications such as those of, for example, CGLI and the RSA. The National

Council for Vocational Qualifications has been doing some work on groups of competences which might be relevant.

The important thing would be to rationalise what is on offer and create a coherent framework within which students could choose. Robustness and clarity are of the essence: one of the aims of any scheme must be to enable the ordinary citizen to grasp, in bold outline, what is on offer. Let us suppose this results in some 20 programme areas. Students would move into activities leading to qualifications in their chosen area. The outcomes would have to make sense: that is, they would have to be useful to the student if they were used as terminal qualifications (and therefore require the blessing of NCVQ) while at the same time being 'progressive', in the sense of keeping open the possibility of further study at a higher level. It would be a matter of debate how far it would be appropriate to insist on what the National Curriculum Council calls a 'whole curriculum framework': there would be a lot to be said for the development of some sort of core to a 'Key Stage 5' – that is, for the 16-18 curriculum – a topic to which we shall return.

It would then be the aim to organise provision in schools and FE colleges so that every 15-16 year old could choose to stay at school to pursue a course in a programme area which could be provided in school; or a programme area which is available in the FE college full-time; or enter employment and combine work with part-time learning within one of the programme areas. The common assumption would be that all students and trainees would continue in education and training at least to 18.

This would mean that there would be:
- two routes for 16-18s (academic and vocational)
- two modes (full-time and part-time)
- overlapping qualifications (A levels and NVQs)
- two sets of destinations (higher education and work).

Expressed baldly there is a danger that some may read into this a rigid distinction between 'academic' and 'vocational' which would be obviously undesirable. Some courses which are now labelled 'academic' are of obvious vocational relevance and some which carry the vocational label can lead on to continued academic study. For the purpose of this discussion, I have in mind the present distinction between courses leading to 'academic' examinations like A levels which come within the framework of the school examinations system, and courses leading to the 'vocational' examinations which come under such bodies as BTEC and City and Guilds.

Every student would be entitled to efficient guidance and this would have to be provided by advisers whose first responsibility was to the student not to a school or college. Counselling for students and their parents would be important in promoting the idea of continuity to 18.

For historical reasons, if for no other, it would be necessary for some programmes to continue to be offered both in school and in FE college. This is untidy. It can lead to confusion; there are bureaucratic difficulties in that schools and FE institutions are administered under different sets of DES Regulations; but the overlap offers the individual more choice and there is no reason to believe that the resulting competition between institutions is other than healthy.

The emphasis should be on what is provided within the 'system' rather than on where it is provided. Both the academic and the vocational routes should be able to lead to qualifications which open the way to higher education or professional recognition. Some of these would be approved as NVQ level III (like BTEC National): others would come into the shadowy category of 'NVQ equivalent'.

The Business and Technician Education Council and its structure of First, National and Higher National qualifications – all available on the basis of full or part-time study – is clearly highly relevant to any rationalisation on these lines. Notwithstanding the difficulties which BTEC has encountered in regard to the National Council for Vocational Qualifications, this structure lines up relatively easily with NVQs.

BTEC is not perfect. No doubt it could be improved. There are those who level criticism against its system of moderating the examinations on which its qualifications are awarded. But BTEC is a well-established organisation with a world-wide reputation. Its National awards are deemed to be acceptable as entry qualifications for higher education. If there is to be a well-defined structure for full-time FE the logical thing to do is to give BTEC a major role. The DES has already invested heavily in BTEC over the years; it would be foolish not to follow the logic of past policy and build on what is in place. The way in which the Scots transformed the Scottish equivalent of BTEC into SCOTVEC and gave it a remit to develop units and modules for further education across the board, provides a powerful example of what can be done in the smaller, more manageable context north of the border: again, not perfect but most impressive all the same. SCOTVEC now has to modify its units to meet Industry Lead Body requirements to conform to the NCVQ model.

The City and Guilds of London Institute, the Royal Society of Arts, and other organisations, with long and valuable records of past service, would also have to be accommodated within a reconstructed English system – accommodated, but not allowed, individually, to veto the kind of rationalisation process which is needed.

How are these changes to be brought about?

The first step should be for the Secretaries of State for Education and Employment to set up a joint Working Group, charged with the initial task of drawing up the new map and setting out the options.

Up till now, there has been no single body capable of looking across the whole range of general and vocational education. Control and guidance are split between two sets of organisations and two Departments of State. For 'academic' education there are the two statutory bodies – the National Curriculum Council (NCC) and the School Examinations and Assessment Council (SEAC) – set up under the Education Reform Act. These advise the Education Secretary on the National Curriculum and its assessment, and on the external GCSE and A and AS level examinations. These bodies have no remit for vocational education and the examination bodies like BTEC and City and Guilds which offer vocational education qualifications. The DES does, of course, have overall responsibility for further education, and the Further Education Unit (FEU) was set up by the DES to engage in curriculum research and development.

Vocational qualifications, on the other hand, come under the National Council for Vocational Qualifications which, though jointly sponsored by the DES and the Department of Employment, is clearly seen as the creature of the DE. It is the government's chosen instrument for giving structured recognition to the acquisition of the skills which industry and commerce value.

This dichotomy reflects, once again, the gap between general and vocational education which lies at the centre of the system: to bridge that gap there has to be a new over-arching body – short-title, say, 'The 14-18 Council' – which can co-ordinate planning for all kinds of courses and qualifications. The immediate task is to create a well-defined set of options which bridge the 16 plus divide and which provide clearly-marked full- and part-time routes for the increasing numbers of students who will stay on to 17 and 18. The long-term aim would be to make general and vocational education complementary elements rather than alternatives. The immediate task is to rationalise and clarify the paths through the years 14 to 18 but this is not to suggest that education and training stops at 18 or that attention should be exclusively concentrated on the initial or 'foundation' stage.

There would still remain quite separate tasks to be performed by the NCC and SEAC for large areas of education in schools, and by NCVQ in accrediting vocational training qualifications. It is not suggested that the existing bodies should merge to form a giant over-arching body with an absurdly wide brief. But for the purpose of bringing order and continuity to the educational needs of the 14-18s it is essential to create an effective organisation for coordinating curriculum and qualifications across the whole range of educational opportunity. In working out the details – and overcoming the undoubted practical problems implicit in creating this hybrid body – the ultimate aim must be kept resolutely in sight: to tackle the historic failure of English education to integrate the academic and the practical, the general and the vocational. Nothing less will meet the challenge of the coming century.

There have been many calls in the past for a single Department of Education and Training, and such a proposal is now being put forward as the policy of the Labour Party. This is not a matter on which opinion need divide on party lines. To set up a single Department would signal a determination at long last to get to grips with what is generally acknowledged to be a cardinal English weakness. But this said, it has also to be recognised that a new Department along these lines would not, in itself, remove the tensions between education and employment. What is essential is to recognise disputes over 'turf' – within or between Departments – for what they are, and not to let them obscure the main task.

Under Section 24 of the Education Reform Act, the Secretary of State for Education has extensive powers to control the curriculum and examinations for all full-time students up the age of 18. He has the authority to decide 'what qualifications authenticated by outside persons' may be provided in FE colleges. If he chooses to use it, he has the same power to control what courses of study are put in place for under-19s in full-time FE as he has for the primary and secondary schools.

These powers have not been used as yet but they were included in the Act in prudent anticipation of a time when it would become possible to review the structure as a whole. They make clear the central role which the DES should play in the process but this does not mean that the DES should necessarily be the senior partner in all matters of vocational education. Here it is the needs of industry and commerce which are deemed to be paramount, and therefore the Department of Employment must have a powerful voice in its own right, and through the National Council for Vocational Qualifications.

The differences in aims and philosophy between the DES-based curriculum and examinations bodies (NCC and SEAC) and the DE-based NCVQ are at the centre of the problem of simplifying and rationalizing the post-16 education system. Not only are there specific differences in working methods and principles, there are also the deep-seated differences in tradition and language which divide the education culture from the training culture. The NCVQ is the articulation of this training culture and this needs to be understood if there is to be any bridging of the Great Divide.

## The National Council for Vocational Qualifications

NCVQ is a relatively new institution – the working group under Oscar De Ville which was set up to review vocational qualifications only reported in 1986[2], following which NCVQ came into being. It is an industry-led body. In a tendentious phrase, industry is seen as the 'owners' of NVQs – the qualifications which receive the NCVQ seal of approval. In practice, industry often means 'employers' because of the determined government efforts since 1979, to keep trade union influence to the minimum.

The Council has adopted a competence-based model for the specification of qualifications. This is a North American import. Competence-Based Education and Training (CBET) had a brief vogue in connection with attempts to reform American teacher-training some twenty years ago, along with short-lived experiments with performance accounting and other attempts to apply a systems approach to teaching and learning. Since then the model has been refined and developed with particular reference to vocational training.[3]

An NVQ is based on a 'statement of competence' in a particular vocational area – that is, a description of what a successful candidate must be able to do to be adjudged capable of exercising the skill which

29

is to be certified. The essence of the approach is that it concentrates on 'outcomes'. Performance is what counts – candidates are assessed on their performance according to the criteria laid down along with the statement of competence. NCVQ is not concerned with courses or institutions or how a candidate acquired the skills which are being assessed: its sole concern is with 'outcomes', a key NVQ word.

The rules are set out in *NVQ Criteria and Procedures (1989).*[4] The statement of competence must incorporate specified standards relating to 'the ability to perform in a range of work-related activities and the underpinning skills, knowledge and understanding required for performance in employment'. Throughout, the various competence requirements are spelled out in terms of what the candidate must be able to do, and to what standard. Even the grammatical form is prescribed to make sure they are as unambiguously linked to measurable performance as possible.

The NCVQ framework provides for five levels: from Level I which certifies competence in routine operations, to Level V which would cover the professions. Level II and III assume progressively more demanding work activities and more individual responsibility. Level III asks for 'competence in skilled areas that involve performance of a broad range of work activities including many that are complex and non-routine'.

The task of setting standards in an area of competence covered by an NVQ is entrusted to an Industry Lead Body, some 130 of which had been set up by 1990. In some cases these are recognised industry training organisations which were already in existence before the inception of NCVQ. Some organisations have been formed to represent the interests of disparate groups as in the case of health and community care. Others are based on trade associations.

Stimulating the formation of Industry Lead Bodies was originally the task of the Department of Employment's Training Agency, which acted as godfather to the NCVQ. Progress has been slower than had been hoped and many of the first NVQs could only be accredited on a conditional basis. Many NVQs are based on existing vocational qualifications awarded by bodies like City and Guilds and the Royal Society of Arts. In other areas like health and community care, new lead bodies have been formed to bring together the range of professional and trade union interests involved.

For reasons which are not difficult to guess, this approach to standard-setting demands major concessions from some of the existing organisations concerned with vocational education. Long and complicated negotiations between BTEC and NCVQ were needed to resolve difficulties arising from the way BTEC courses were validated – they allowed a degree of independent initiative to the colleges which the NCVQ was reluctant to accept. BTEC, for its part, was uncomfortable with the proliferation of qualifications to meet the specific needs of an increasing number of 'owners'. It preferred its own method of consulting employers and translating their views into vocational education procedures, evaluating their views and providing national guidelines within which education and training providers can meet more specific needs. In the view of NCVQ this had not led to the establishment of national standards. It was not till the autumn of 1990, that a treaty between the two organisations was formally concluded, paving the way for some 200,000 BTEC students to gain a qualification within the NCVQ framework each year from 1992 onwards provided that the agreement holds and can be made to work in practice. Part of the deal required the reformulation of BTEC programmes in line with the competences defined by Lead Bodies in each major industry served by BTEC qualifications. The terms are intended to allow them to retain the breadth which they need if they are to continue to offer a ladder to higher education.[5]

The NCVQ documentation recognises the need for breadth in the specification of competence, but there has been widespread concern that some Industry Lead Bodies have formulated their skill requirements too narrowly. The concept of competence in performance, assessed where possible in the work-place, puts great emphasis on measurable, behavioural changes. The rhetoric tends to be all about doing rather than knowing. Yet the guidelines clearly stipulate that competence includes the knowledge and understanding needed to back up specific skills.

There is no inherent reason why a competence-based model should be inconsistent with the specification of an extensive knowledge base. In theory, too, a wide range of 'process' skills like scientific method or the capacity for independent critical inquiry can also be demanded as outcomes and their performance can be measured in specified ways. But this has not been how most Industry Lead Bodies have so far interpreted the notion of NVQs. There is an obvious tension between the employers' immediate shop-floor demands and the wider need to give trainees the background which can make them versatile and able to survive changes in occupational requirements. In the first phase it looks as if the immediate shop-floor demands won.

Competence is not only about skills, knowledge and understanding – it also concerns other personal qualities and attitudes. These too can be defined and exemplified in specified forms of action. But the more closely competence is examined, elaborated and refined – as a concept and in practice – the less transparent it becomes. It invites endless jargon and quickly loses the bluff simplicity which at first sight is its great attraction.[6]

In the attempt to maintain a broad concept of competence, the NCVQ has broached the idea of 'generic' units which would incorporate skills which are complementary to more specific forms of competence. But it is, perhaps, symptomatic of the underlying tension that progress on these and related matters seems to have lagged.

The NCVQ insistence on limiting its concerns to specified, measurable, outcomes has some important pragmatic virtues for further education generally (to which we will return). But that is not the whole story. The theories behind competence-based education and training and the rules which NCVQ has made to put the theories into practice have a powerful effect on defining what is regarded as important and, therefore, what people should learn. The methods and the rules are presented as if they were self-evidently right – as if this is obviously the best way to operate. But it is quite clear that this is not self-evidently so: it is notable, for example, that West Germany, the European country that seems to be most successful in vocational education and training, has not adopted CBET or the psychology on which it is founded. The mix of knowledge, understanding and skills with which the West Germans equip their young workers is richer than British employers have demanded. Researchers at the National Institute of Economic and Social Research have argued that there is a link between the quality of the education and training of young German workers and the level of sophistication of German industrial activity – the ability of the German labour force to produce goods with high added value.

All this needs to be borne in mind in considering the role of NCVQ in relation to vocational education. The Council has not been directly concerned up till now with vocational education – only with vocational *qualifications.* Yet the NCVQ's version of CBET has now become, in effect, the official ideology of British vocational education and training. Like all official ideologies it needs to be regarded with a due measure of suspicion.[7]

**The clash of cultures**

It has long been part of the rhetoric to claim that education and training belong to a single continuum which runs from the most academic learning at one end to the clearest forms of training at the other. But the separate terms 'education' and 'training' describe differences which are real, not imaginary. The NCVQ belongs clearly at the 'training' end of the continuum: its methods and principles are derived directly from the imperatives of training: its culture, as we have noted, is a training culture.

Educational institutions, on the other hand, are the product of a different culture. This shows in widespread suspicion of the National Council for Vocational Qualifications in some educational circles (though not, it should be said, in further education). And not without reason if all you go by is the language and rhetoric in which NCVQ chooses to clothe its ideas, and the scarcely-veiled conviction of some of its leading officials that its methodology and philosophy are what are needed to reform secondary education.[8]

Everyone in education is familiar with the reductionist dangers of 'teaching to the test'. Yet in its forthright way, the NCVQ seems to have elevated the idea of 'teaching to the test' to the level of a supreme principle. It insists that all that is needful can be set out in the statement of competence and the assessment criteria. It must be obvious that carried to its logical conclusion this could devalue the *processes* of organised teaching and learning which are the business of schools and colleges.

Education is not a mechanical process. The same experience will lead different pupils to different outcomes. That is why there is no such thing as a 'teacher-proof' curriculum – the philosopher's stone that mechanistic curriculum developers in the United States searched for in vain in the 1960s. No matter how clearly the outcomes are planned in advance, the best education remains – and ought to remain – to an important extent open-ended. Tim Eggar, Minister of State at the DES, made this point himself indirectly in an interview with David Tytler of *The Times* shortly after he took up his job.[9] Reflecting on his own, 'immensely privileged' education at Winchester, he said: 'The thing I remember is the whole time being made to think things out for oneself'. It is fairly safe to say that the horizons his schoolmasters opened up for him were not foreshortened by any pre-determined list of prescribed behavioural outcomes. Many would doubt he would have benefited if they had been.

The late Alec Clegg, the last chief education officer for the West Riding of Yorkshire, used to distinguish between pot-filling and fire-lighting. CBET looks like a relatively efficient way of encouraging and assessing pot-filling, but the educational consequences would be undesirable if it made fire-lighting an act of supererogation – a distraction from prescribed tasks.

Put like this, the gulf between the two cultures seems wide. In practice, the gap between the NCVQ and the two institutions created by the Education Reform Act to oversee the National Curriculum is narrower than it might seem. The National Curriculum is also based on the specification of 'outcomes' in the form of Attainment Targets. The thinking behind the National Curriculum is utilitarian and instrumentalist. Its outcomes do not, however, stand alone. They are not regarded as the only important element. The National Curriculum is fleshed out in terms of activities – the 'programmes of study' which are required – as well as the assessment criteria. And the National Curriculum exists within the context of schools which are part of the education culture, not the training culture.

There is no reason why the two great engines of control – NCVQ for vocational qualifications and SEAC/NCC for the school curriculum and examinations – should not achieve a genuine meeting of minds and produce answers that draw constructively on both traditions and both cultures.

Further education is ideally suited to be the test-bed for a new approach to vocational education which benefits from the clarity and sharpness of the NCVQ's skills approach, without losing sight of the process concerns which have traditionally been regarded as important by the educators.

What is clear is that much of the input will have to come from the NCVQ. If vocational education in FE colleges (and, in some school courses in, for example, business studies) are to have currency in the wider world it is essential that they should fit into an NCVQ framework.

The problem is that, at the moment, the NCVQ framework has been constructed with trainees in employment, mainly, in mind. It may well be necessary for a new range of 'Associate NVQs' to be created for some full-time college-based students. These would include units and modules which are common to the NVQs developed for work-based trainees, but would equip the student with a wider background knowledge and would therefore do more to keep open options for progression.

On entering employment, FE students with 'Associate NVQs' would have most of what would be required for an ordinary NVQ. They would be the natural beneficiaries of the great importance NCVQ already gives to the 'recognition of prior achievement' – one of the consequences of defining competence solely in terms of performance is that anyone who can demonstrate the competence is entitled to the qualification.

Clearly what is needed is a genuine cooperative effort between NCVQ and SEAC, not just the exercise in power play that is all too likely to occur. Real difficulties will have to be overcome because of the suspicion that the DES is dominated by 'school' assumptions and because the NCVQ is a body which has expressly eschewed any interest in vocational *education* to concentrate on vocational *qualifications.*

If NCVQ were to create its own 'Associate NVQ' qualifications, control of the content could not remain with the Industry Lead Bodies. They should continue to be consulted and to have a powerful influence but their role should be modified in such a way as to leave to 'The 14-18 Council' the final say in deciding what combination of knowledge, understanding and skills should be pursued in any programme area. In this sense, the employers' 'ownership' of the qualification would be called in question. The point is that the balance needs to be negotiated in such a way as to take account of the wider interests of society, and of the individual, as well as those of the employers.

**Progression to higher education**
Ideally, the pattern of provision at 16-18 should hold out the widest possibility for students who take the vocational path to qualify for higher and professional education later on. To make this point is sometimes seen as yet another expression of the elitist obsession – the same obsession which has (in the view of many critics) diverted FE from its main task which is to provide high quality intermediate education in vocational skills. There is, certainly, a temptation for colleges to pursue the prestige attached to preparing students for university and polytechnic entrance: in an increasingly competitive

and entrepreneurial environment, there is a real risk of this leading to the neglect of other responsibilities. But the ladder must be in place and represent a genuine alternative route as, for example, by way of BTEC, to degree and Higher National Certificate and Diploma courses. Otherwise a reform along these lines would be a fraud and a deception.

There is also the example of the American community colleges to draw on. Such colleges have as one of their commitments the provision of courses that offer students the first two years of a first degree. The aim is to provide a cheap and convenient way in which students can make a start on a first degree locally and at low cost. The universities need to be assured that the courses offered by the community colleges meet their requirements. If they do they will accept 'transfer' students and give them credit for the work they have done.

Further Education Colleges already run 'Access' courses for students who want to go to university or polytechnic or college of higher education but lack background knowledge, confidence and study skills. A logical extension of the idea of Access courses has been the linking of FE colleges with a university or polytechnic to enable a degree course to be begun at college. Among the successful examples are the scheme based on the University of Lancaster in the north-west of England, and the Mundella scheme at the University of Sheffield. The Sheffield scheme, funded in part by the Training Agency, enables a number of colleges in South Yorkshire to offer an informatics course, leading over several years to a certificate (first year), diploma (second year) and eventually a degree, with transfer, if desired, to study in the University. Plans have been made for the extension of the scheme to a group of colleges across the Pennines.[10]

Schemes of this kind emphasise the value of an effective system of credit accumulation and transfer of the kind which has been developed by the Council for National Academic Awards.

It is important to envisage a world in which definitions – of higher education and of entry qualifications – are widened. If we are to talk about a future in which Britain begins to approach the notion of mass higher education, this will certainly not come about without including within the ambit of higher education many forms of advanced vocational and professional training which are not now within the narrow British definition but which will link up directly with NVQ level III.

Much of the current discussion takes place on the false assumption that there is a single standard of entry to higher education now. This is not so – Cambridge mathematics undergraduates have to have three or four As at A level; some colleges of higher education will take in students with two Es in any subject. The Open University has no rigid entry requirement; and there are widening opportunities for many other 'unqualified' adults who can show reasons why they should be admitted. The range of entry qualifications will become wider still if and when (as Christopher Ball would have it) 'more means different' and the definitions of higher education are broadened.[11]

One of the attractions of the way the French have broadened the *baccalaureat* examinations to take in a wider range of vocational education students lies in the fact that they will all, technically, be qualified for entry into higher education. This will not mean, of course, as the CBI Task Force seemed to think, that all those who achieve the French vocational baccalaureat will have achieved a qualification of A Level standard. But it will give successful students access to some courses in some higher education institution. We need to be no less bold. The point is not to try to suggest that every student is going to end up as a graduate, nor yet that getting students into university or polytechnic should be the only aim that counts for an FE college, but simply to keep the avenues of opportunity open for as many as possible, as long as possible – to build, in fact, an open system.

Some full-time students will, no doubt, continue to drop out at 17 armed with whatever modules of general and vocational education and NVQ units they have been able to acquire. It will, in any case, become increasingly difficult to make sharp distinctions between full- and part-time students – more and more will need to work to maintain themselves on allegedly full-time courses. Others will continue to take advantage of the 21-hour rule (which future governments may have the wisdom to interpret more generously). Already, the 'contact-time' – time in classes – enjoyed by some full-time students may be less than that for some part-timers.

## A common core

Attention has focussed recently on the question of a core of common skills for 16-18 year-olds. Is it possible to identify a set of skills which should be taught to all students and trainees in this age-group, in school, college and in private sector training organisations? The idea of such a core is attractive because it might provide a unifying element in a 16 to 18 curriculum; it might serve as one of the means by which, on the one hand, to counter the tendency of some Industry Lead Bodies to concentrate too narrowly on specific skills and, on the other, to broaden the narrow remit of the traditional sixth-form course.

The response to John MacGregor's initiative on core skills in the autumn of 1989 has been encouraging: NCC, SEAC, NCVQ, FEU and the Training Agency have found little difficulty in working closely together and reaching a wide measure of agreement.[12]

This is not a new discussion. One possible approach is to reach down into the western cultural tradition and come up with a definition of the hard core of general education which every citizen should have. One version of this approach could be seen in the FEU's *A Basis for Choice* (1979); its latest manifestation can be seen in the interest aroused recently in the United States by E.D. Hirsch's *Cultural Literacy* (1987). In earlier generations this craving for a common cultural repertoire was to be seen in the development of general studies courses intended to civilise science students or give humanities students a smattering of the history of science.

Others believed that a core could be found by abstracting the skills that are common to a wide range of tasks – skills which, therefore, are transferable between occupations. It is this second approach that has been gathering support.

Early in the 1980s, the Manpower Services Commission had picked up work done by the Canadian Department of Manpower and Immigration on generic transferable skills: the inculcation of such skills was included among the early aims of YTS.

Other bodies had begun to move in the same direction. A core of related knowledge, skills, qualities and attitudes has featured in the requirements of BTEC, the TVEI, and the Certificate of Pre-Vocational Education. Not all have assumed exactly the same core but there has been a large measure of agreement. An HMI paper[13] noted 10 elements which recurred frequently:

- Knowledge about information technology
- Using information technology
- Knowledge about industry and commerce
- Knowledge about society and the environment
- Communication
- Numeracy
- Problem-solving
- Practical skills

- Working cooperatively
- Adaptability

The CBI Task Force also wanted education and training to develop a mixture of moral virtues and positive attitudes ('values and integrity', and 'positive attitudes to change') along with practical skills like 'effective communication', 'applications of numeracy' and 'problem-solving'.

In his ACFHE speech, Kenneth Baker added his own selection:
- Communication
- Numeracy
- Personal relations (teamwork etc)
- Familiarity with technology
- Familiarity with systems
- Familiarity with changing working and social contexts (eg Europe, 1992 etc)

The National Curriculum Council concluded that

> Communication, problem-solving and personal skills should be incorporated in all post-16 programmes and embedded in every A and AS syllabus.

> Numeracy, information technology and modern language competence cannot be fully developed in every subject, although there is more scope for the first two than the third. Aspects of numeracy and information technology which match A and AS subjects should be embedded in syllabuses'.[14]

Anyone with any knowledge of earlier debates on continuing education will find it odd (as would many overseas observers) that 'citizenship' finds no place in the list of core skills or cross-curricular themes. In the contemporary environment citizenship has no market value.

The NCC worked closely with the NCVQ and the Further Education Unit on core skills and agreed to cooperate in a joint programme of development. Gilbert Jessup, the research director of NCVQ and architect of its methodology, also published a paper setting out the NCVQ view which fully supported the idea of

> ...a common set of core skills which could be incorporated in both A/AS levels and post-16 curriculum in schools on the one hand, and in NVQs or as units within the NVQ framework, on the other.'[15]

The NCC had linked the idea to a single national record of achievement. This also ties up with NCVQ thinking. Jessup maintained that the common core skills should be specified, in the NVQ manner, as outcomes not inputs, thus enabling them to be assessed without reference to any particular course. He was chary of 'bolt-on' additions aimed at adding particular core skills, preferring that the skills should be embedded in existing subjects. (BTEC has practised and refined this approach since the early 1980s.) In the back of everyone's mind is the recollection of past attempts to teach 'general studies' to reluctant apprentices and a profound conviction that if there is to be a serious attempt to broaden and strengthen the curriculum across the board it must be done by enriching the existing content rather than by prescribing additional courses or modules which will appear to the student to be irrelevant.

On the other hand two of the elements of the common core which seem to achieve most consensual support – problem-solving and personal social skills – are fraught with difficulty. The Training Agency believes that recent research can be adduced to support the claims of both, but as with the teaching of 'thinking skills' (another claimant for time and attention which last year was the subject of an international conference at OECD in Paris) there are many who harbour unresolved doubts about transfer – the application of skills acquired in one context in different circumstances.[16]

SEAC's response has been to press ahead, with the other organisations concerned, with the work necessary for the inclusion of core skills in A and AS level examinations in 1994. The aim would be to make sure the prescribed common skills – which are said to be already required by many existing syllabuses – are made explicit to the students and are duly assessed. A similar exercise by NCVQ will be undertaken with a view to making it a requirement that problem-solving, communication, and personal skills are built into all NVQs and encouraging the inclusion of the other core skills – numeracy, information technology and modern language competence – in NVQs by Industry Lead Bodies.

There has been a general readiness to explore ways in which the core skills exercise could be used to encourage credit transfer, including the linkage of A and AS levels with vocational qualifications by developing common modules of study. SEAC and NCVQ are looking at the overlap which may be possible in seven areas including business studies, science, English, modern languages and design and technology and this will support efforts already going on to promote common units of study across different courses. Everything suggests that the drive towards modular course design is going to gather strength post-16. This will make it easier to achieve a much greater degree of mixing of the vocational and the academic than has been possible up to now.

Can the work on core skills go on to create a recognisable core curriculum for 'Key Stage 5'? It is important that there should be formal requirements for 'communication' and 'numeracy' (English and maths – why be coy?) along with IT and a continued modern language element. It will not be enough to say this is difficult: it will be a test of whether we are serious in what is said about joining the world class or not. Our hand will be forced by the rest of the Western world which expects to have a literate, numerate, IT-competent, workforce.

## 14 to 16 to 18

If the intention is to devise a scheme that really does treat 14 to 18 as a single span, it would be essential to follow the logic that has been at work in TVEI and which has been picked up by the CBI Task Force. This means broadening the current discussion of Key Stage 4 in the national curriculum to have regard to the need to promote continuity beyond 16.

It has already become clear that the 10-subject curriculum set out in Section 3 of the Education Reform Act presents the planners with formidable problems. It was already conceded by John MacGregor, in his speech to the Society of Education Officers in January 1990, that there would have to be some differentiation at this stage when pupils decide which subjects to take for GCSE. There is talk of half-subjects and other less time-consuming ways of satisfying the legal requirements of the national curriculum.

Kenneth Clarke carried the process of revision a stage further, defining a 5-subject extended core for the 14 to 16 year-olds, consisting of English, mathematics, science, technology and a modern language. Outside this core area, there is to be flexibility to accommodate, for example, pupils who want to take the three separate science subjects, add a second or third modern language, or study the classics. This same flexibility will be used to enable some pupils to start on the vocational route (via BTEC) before the age of 16.

This will mean a break with present practice which will be fiercely attacked in some quarters as a retreat from the ideals of comprehensive education. But the facts about truancy and absenteeism in the final years of the compulsory period speak for themselves. By the age of 14 many pupils have been turned off and, if not wholly alienated, are by no means enthusiastic learners of the traditional school subjects. It is an illusion to believe that a tightly prescribed knowledge-based National Curriculum is going to change this if the other, external, causes of alienation and absenteeism remain. It has been forcefully argued by Sig Prais and others that one reason why some continental school systems appear to have more success with sections of the school community which fail in England is because they are more ready to accept that pupils learn in different ways and to start some pupils on vocational courses before 16.[17] Such a development should not be excluded as an option in this country provided that the need to keep things in perspective is recognised.

The main aim should be to produce connected learning opportunities which carry more students through from 14 to 18 and enable them to achieve more. Far from being regarded as a way of depriving any boy or girl of opportunities for general education, giving some of them the chance to learn through the medium of realistic vocational studies should be seen as an attempt to extend their potential for learning in ways to which they may better respond, and within a framework which still allows for the possibility of progression. It is not just a matter of the content of the work the students undertake. It is also how they are treated, the ethos of the course and the attitudes it promotes, the relevance of work experience and the provision of individual action plans and learning schemes.

Nobody would suggest that all problems of motivation are going to be solved by allowing some 14 and 15 year-olds to start down the vocational route. But it would make sense to try to encourage an expectation of continuing vocational education beyond school and into employment and to use this to generate practical interest.

In this, the experience gained through the Technical and Vocational Education Initiative should be directly relevant. So, too, should the curriculum development which is taking place in the first City Technology Colleges. The way in which the CTCs were brought into existence makes it difficult for the maintained schools and FE Colleges to benefit from their experience, but when the political dust settles it would be foolish not to recognise that (albeit in privileged circumstances) the CTCs are confronting many of the same problems that face all the schools in encouraging pupils to achieve the success which carries them through to 18. Labour's election plans envisage the incorporation of the CTCs within the local authority system: if this happens it will be important not to waste what is being learned at Kingshurst and the other nascent colleges.

## GCSE and A levels

So long as success in GCSE – crudely measured in the public mind as five subjects at grade A-C – is seen as the minimum passport to the sixth form, GCSE must also be seen as defining who should leave at the earliest possible age. As it stands, GCSE is a gate-keeper and carries out the negative functions of a gate-keeper all too effectively. It is true that GCSE looks like letting a few more through the gate than GCE and CSE but it still certifies failure on a grand scale.

And A levels as now conceived define the road to higher education in extremely narrow terms. Moreover, it is still (to some extent at least) a norm-referenced examination: there is a built in assumption that many candidates will fail – up to a third each year.

The merits of A levels lie in the demands they make on the select band of students who submit themselves for examination, and the quality of the work generated by the best specialised A level teaching in schools and FE colleges alike. Till now, this has been combined with the assumption that only the abler members of this elite group come up to the rigorous demands of university and polytechnic entrance. The consequence has been to create the kind of social pressures which enable teachers to demand total commitment – some of the students will work harder for their A levels than at any subsequent time in their lives. Similar social pressure can produce a similar commitment, as in the case of students working for admission to the Grandes Écoles in France, or the Royal Universities in Japan.

If this commitment is a conspicuous virtue in the A level system, it is important also to recognise the equally conspicuous demerits. These include the degree of excessive specialisation which gives the English sixth-form its peculiar character, and the effect which this narrowly-defined upper storey – with all its rigour – has on the rest of the educational structure. Education before the sixth form becomes a method of sifting the chaff to provide the graded grains to go into the A level mill. And in the context of the present discussion, the dominant role of A levels effectively prevents the due recognition of the vocational route. In so doing it restricts choice and individual fulfilment.

The rejection of the Higginson proposals out of hand left the future of the school sixth forms as an outstanding item on the agenda. The paramount need is to clean the bath without swilling the baby down the plughole. It will require enormous finesse. The introduction of AS levels can be regarded only as tinkering with the larger problem which should now be considered within the framework of a review of 14-18 as a whole. As at present organised, the sixth-form curriculum becomes increasingly unsatisfactory and the need for change has been widely recognised by 'users' of the sixth-form product, both in the universities and in industry.

One logical response to the manifest shortcomings and negative effects of the GCSE and A levels is to demand a clean sweep of the present system of external academic exams and the substitution of a new baccalaureat-type examination at 18, covering the full range of activities in general and vocational education. The French example shows one way in which this could be done.

*A British Baccalaureat*, the policy paper from the Institute of Public Policy Research, takes this view. This is the logical root-and-branch approach and most people who work in further education would probably support it, if offered a clean sheet on which to redesign the education system.

The question is what to do if you don't start with a *tabula rasa*. The educational scene comprises the institutions and the curriculum structures of 150 years of history and these institutions and structures have been endowed with great and mysterious significance within the culture. A levels have developed within the context of an elite higher education system for which they provide part of the underpinning. They are guarantors of quality and high standards for the kind of three-year first degree that England takes for granted.

The need for an enlarged concept of higher education has already been referred to. Without wider definitions it will not be possible to make sense of the kind of expansion envisaged for the future. It is obvious that this must entail big changes in examining at 18. The question is: are these changes (which will be needed over a period of time and not necessarily all at once) easier to negotiate by means of a 'Big Bang' or by building incrementally on developments which are already in hand?

My own preference is for the latter for reasons which are practical, not ideological. (They may also be temperamental.) I am highly sceptical about revolutionary change in education, given the limited pace at which individuals and institutions can respond and the virtual certainty that any root-and-branch change will be underfunded.

Many people, including a former Education Secretary, Shirley Williams,[18] have claimed that the common sense of the argument points at some future stage to the elimination of GCSE in its present form. This has all along been a logical corollary to the assessment procedures being built into the National Curriculum. If all 14-year-old students are going to stay in education, full- or part-time, till they are 18 it makes little sense to have this kind of make-or-break external examination at 16.

But, this said, it has to be acknowledged that the 16 plus examination has only recently been reviewed and reorganised. Its credibility has been painfully defended against the critics on the hard right who hark back to the good old days of the School Certificate and the London matric. A premature attempt to change what has just been brought in at great political and professional cost would seriously prejudice other aspects of the reform of 14 to 18 education. By the end of the century, the GCSE will be made redundant by the assessment apparatus of the National Curriculum. But that is some way ahead. In the meantime it may well be more productive to work on opening up access to BTEC as an alternative basis for progression beyond 16 – one which bypasses the narrow gate and gives explicit recognition to the concerns of pupils whose interests will take them along the vocational route. To maintain the emphasis on a 14 to 18 span, the examinations at 16 – academic and vocational – should adopt the term 'Intermediate'.

So long as GCSE does remain it will continue to be seen as a qualifying exam for full-time education post-16. It will be important to counter this head on, by developing action plans for students which cross the divide at 16, which are not dependent on a minimum of four or five GCSEs at Grades A to C and make good gaps in previous learning without simply prescribing GCSE 'retakes' as a matter of routine. This reinforces the need for much improved guidance and counselling services.

## A tertiary structure

The creation of a well-designed system of education for the 16-18s would require every LEA to make their plans so that a full range of programme areas can be offered to every pupil, in school or in FE. Each student would have to be helped to arrive at an individual action plan which would represent his negotiated menu selection. Most LEAs would have to organise what was on offer in a tertiary system composed of schools and colleges together.

The term 'tertiary' is not ideal to describe the range of provision for 16 to 19s, but it has now gained a general currency and a number of local education authorities have created tertiary colleges – FE colleges which provide the full range of full- and part-time courses which might otherwise be organised separately in school sixth forms and FE colleges. The indications are that these include many first-rate institutions which enjoy strong support among parents and students.

It is not practical to imagine a wholesale reorganisation on tertiary college lines, but where and if reorganisation becomes necessary it would be logical to think in tertiary terms. Given the individualistic nature of schools as institutions and the competitive edge which has been sharpened by local management, much thought would have to be given to ways of making tertiary planning a reality for the consumer.

In some FE colleges there may be a strong case for hiving off the 'tertiary' work by creating a 'tertiary college within a college'. Members of the FE community are ambivalent about this: on the one hand they recognise their responsibilities to their younger students; on the other they want to present their institutions as adult communities and this is not made easier by the presence of a large contingent of teenagers. One answer is to treat the teenagers as a coherent group and give them their own space. But against this there is the wish to treat the 16-18 year-olds as adults and to integrate them in the larger community.

## Apprenticeship

The people for whom it is going to continue to be most difficult to guarantee a square deal in the matter of vocational education and training are clearly still going to be those who go straight into employment at 16. Reference has already been made to the article by Richard Layard and Sig Prais in which they argued the case for compulsion – going back to earlier plans for making continued part-time education obligatory for young school-leavers, and making it illegal for employers to hire under-18s except as trainees.

John Cassels' answer in *Britain's Real Skill Shortage* was to lay no compulsion on the young but make it a statutory requirement that contracts of employment for 16-18 year-olds 'must provide for structured training on and off the job leading to a recognised qualification at age 18' or be rendered null and void. (He also wanted all government funding for training costs to be paid on condition that trainees' wages were restricted to allowances controlled by the Department of Employment in order to bring down the costs of employment for trainees. This echoes one of the strengths of the German system.)

Labour policy documents promise a statutory framework which will include a replacement for YTS in the shape of 'a new training guarantee – a traineeship lasting for up to four years and leading to qualifications recognised throughout Britain and the rest of Europe.' (*Looking to the Future*). Another Labour Party paper, *Investing in Britain's Future*, refers to a 'new four year technical and vocational traineeship which would have a significant educational component... predominantly education-based in its first two years and employer-based in the final two years'.

These are all, in their different ways, attempts to provide statutory backing for the universalisation of vocational education and training for the under-19s. The case for putting youth training on some sort of a legal basis is already very strong. Most people will see the CBI Task Group's report as the last attempt to show industry can do what is necessary without the intervention of Parliament. If it fails, legislation will surely have to follow: if it succeeds, there may still need to be legislation to tie up the loose ends.

Even if Parliament eschews coercive legislation, there must, even so, be a strong case for creating formal structures within which the employers' enlightened self-interest can come to fruition. Those who leave full-time education and enter employment at 16 will need a convincing guarantee of the quality of the 'education and training leading to a recognised qualification' which, on paper, the CBI proposals promise them. If this guarantee is not provided under statute, the employers will have to set up their own effective mechanisms: they will have to give trainees a simple but effective training contract and set up their own apparatus for self-regulation in order to make good their side of the bargain.

If trainee status is to be given full meaning within the community (as it must be, if the cultural sea-change which the CBI scheme is banking on is to have any chance of becoming a reality), there would have to be some kind of national inspectorate to monitor standards and watch the public interest. Large sums of public money are going to continue to flow into training and Parliament can only know how this is being spent if there is an efficient watchdog.

It is important to resurrect the idea of organised training as what the French call *formation* – more than just the inculcation of specific skills, a sustained experience which is intended to build character as well as competence. The implication would be that someone who had been through a period of planned training would have acquired the necessary knowledge, understanding and skill to perform effectively as a person, as well as a worker. One of the strengths of the German system must be that it is not just about training for a narrow skill, but about the formation of the adult worker-citizen. Somehow the same ambitious idea has to be built into the CBI's notion of 'careership'.

If a 'national apprenticeship' were set up with its own rules and with high standards built in, it would suggest a deliberate attempt to intervene nationally – to do more, in fact, than just leave it to the market. 'National' apprentices might be an elite body, possibly recruited at mainly 17, but not excluding entrants who might come (like the increasing number of German *gymnasium* students who enter the German apprenticeship system) after completing a school or college course to 18.

While there clearly can be no attempt to replicate the arrangements that have been adopted in any other country, it must make sense to learn what we can from Europe and not to be dazzled by American examples just because the free market aura appeals to current ideological enthusiasms. Some sort of national apprenticeship system with terms and conditions and education and training guarantees laid down nationally is necessary if the full vocational education and training revolution at the foundation level is to be achieved.

### Notes

1. *Statistical Bulletin 1/90: International Statistical Comparisons of the Education and Training of 16 to 18 year olds*, DES, London 1990.
2. Review of Vocational Qualifications in England and Wales, MSC and DES, London, 1986.

3. I am greatly indebted to Gilbert Jessup's *Outcomes: NVQs and the Emerging Model of Education and Training*, Falmer Press, London, 1991.

4. See Jessup, op.cit.

5. Details of the agreement were released in a press announcement dated 3 October 1990.

6. See John W. Burke (editor), *Competence Based Education and Training*, Falmer Press, London, 1989.

7. 'The transition towards a competence-based model can be traced through a number of government White Papers throughout the 1980s. *The New Training Initiative* in 1981 set out the philosophy and advocated "standards of a new kind". This was reinforced in White Papers in 1984 and 1985 and *Working Together: Education and Training*, 1986, introduced the framework of national vocational qualifications to operationalise the new model of education and training. The move towards competence based education and training was further reinforced by *Employment for the 1990s* (1988)' – from the Foreword to Burke (editor), op.cit.

8. The most effective exponent of these views is Dr Gilbert Jessup, the Director of Research, Development and Information at NCVQ.

9. *The Times*, 13 August 1990.

10. Peter Duff, Neil Sellors and Alan Walker, *The Mundella Programme: Outreach Higher Education in the Field of Information Studies and Technology*, a report to the Training Agency, Policy Studies Centre, University of Sheffield.

11. Sir Christoper Ball, *More Means Different*, Industry Matters, RSA, London 1990.

12. The Secretary of State's letter of 28 November 1989 refers.

13. HMI Paper, 'Post-16 Education and Training – Core Skills', DES, 1989.

14. National Curriculum Council, *Core Skills 16-19*, NCC, 1990.

15. Gilbert Jessup, *Common Learning Outcomes: Core Skills in A/AS Levels and NVQ*, R&D Report No.6, NCVQ, 1990.

16. See Stuart Maclure, 'The Teaching of Thinking', OECD *Observer*, October-November 1990 and report of OECD Conference on 'Learning to Think: Thinking to Learn' held in Paris in the summer of 1989 (forthcoming from Pergamon Press).

17. Geoff Mason, S.J. Prais and Bart van Ark, *Vocational Education and Productivity in the Netherlands and Britain*, Discussion Paper

No.191, National Institute of Economic and Social Research, November 1990.
18. Shirley Williams, *A Job to Live*, pp.165-166, Penguin Books, London, 1985.

# 3 New Colleges for Old

**How do the colleges need to change to meet the new demands upon them?**
Much of what has been discussed up to now in these pages has concerned the 16 to 19 age group and the clear need to put in place a reliable system of education and training for them which has been highlighted in the CBI proposals. Such a system is needed if the historic failure of English education to provide an effective, complementary, programme of general and vocational education is ever to be made good. The colleges of further education have a key role to play in this.

Vocational education is a priority concern both for full- and part-time students. But FE is not simply, or even primarily, about the 16 to 19s. Indeed, it is characteristic of those who teach in FE colleges to be passionately committed to working with adults in an adult institution: they find their most challenging tasks in teaching those who have missed out on formal education, but who decide to return to systematic study as mature students. It is necessary to get away from narrow age-related conventions about what people learn when and to meet people's needs as and when they become aware of them. Much of the colleges' work in vocational, adult and community education is geared to these adult needs and expectations.

What links all the activities of further education is the voluntary principle: FE offers services to students aged 16 and over. Nobody attends under compulsion. If the CBI succeeds in eliminating employment for young people which does not include a guarantee of structured vocational education and training leading to a recognised qualification, there will, it is true, be strong social pressure on the young to participate. But as of now – and in the immediate future –

FE depends on attracting students by the quality of what it offers. The further education colleges have to be attractive places, projecting a public reputation and an image which make people want to take advantage of their services.

'Image' and 'Marketing' are topics which have been high on the FE agenda in recent years. The MSC and the Training Agency have bombarded the colleges with advice and encouragement. The language is the language of commerce – about how to woo their customers and how to adapt their ways to make the colleges more user-friendly. There has been a determined and in some measure successful effort to persuade colleges to look at themselves from the customer's point of view.

It is, of course, impossible to generalise about 400 colleges, each at a different stage in the metamorphosis; for every outstanding example of a college which has completely overhauled its ways of working to become a 'responsive college',[1] there are many more which have yet to respond. But there are now a number of clear pointers as to the kind of open and flexible college which is needed – openness and flexibility being characteristics which have to be tailored to particular local circumstances and markets.

Changing the internal organisation of colleges and turning them into institutions which put the interests of learners first, requires strong professional direction and a willingness on the part of the teaching staff to rethink their jobs from scratch. Some examples of what this can mean are given at the end of this chapter.

## Premises

Changing a college's image also depends on the physical structure of the college itself. Kenneth Baker used the word 'dowdy' to characterise the FE college buildings.

Here again generalisation has to allow for the exceptions, the relatively small number of newly-formed colleges in modern buildings which can be found dotted around the country. The majority of colleges, however, are not bright and new – they are in old buildings which often enough have already outlived their useful lives in some other capacity. Many have been poorly maintained. Local education authorities have consistently skimped on painting and decoration. Maintenance is the item which is easiest to cut when an authority is struggling to balance its budget. Often poor maintenance is compounded by false economies in cleaning. This too contributes to the colleges' image as 'second choice' institutions.

To be attractive to students – all kinds of students – and to the employers whose business the colleges must win, the colleges clearly need a face lift. The sums of money are not likely to be large in relation to the number of the colleges and the capital value of the plant but in absolute terms there can be no doubt the colleges need to have a lot of money spent on them to bring them up to standard. It is not necessary to spend it all at once but there will have to be a 10-year capital programme to put the buildings in order and reshape the further education system to perform the enhanced role which must now be filled.

Just as public companies look closely at the circumstances in which they meet their customers, so too the colleges have to look at the front they present to the public. What sort of an entrance hall? What is it like to wait in the waiting room? Does the college project an image of confidence and success? Are there suitable rooms where staff can meet local employers in civilised surroundings? Can the college caterers produce a decent cup of coffee? How does the college deal with telephone inquiries? Are the telephonists trained to be as helpful as they can be? Is there the right mix of academic staff available in sufficient numbers to deal with the queries from people wanting to find out about courses? If the college pulls out all the stops with a vigorous marketing campaign, can it cope efficiently and in a friendly manner with the interest thus generated?

The whole question of the college's image is basic to any attempt to market the college's activities more aggressively. Matters which are trivial in themselves, when taken together become powerful positive or negative factors in a college's relationship with the public. Many, but not by any means all, of these come back to the state of the buildings.

There ought to be an immediate survey of the present state of the FE estate. There is spare capacity within the FE system, some of which can be absorbed and adapted for future needs. It is one of the ironies of the present time that many colleges have the space to take in more students if their budgets would allow. Amalgamation and consolidation will continue to reduce the number of colleges – the present 400 could come down to something like 250 over the next five or six years.

The colleges need a substantial building programme if they are to be enabled to play a strong and developing role in the 1990s and beyond. Many buildings need to be replaced and extensively remodelled. There is also a need for a minor works programme which would give the colleges themselves the chance to make small but significant improvements without waiting for approval for major projects. The longer improvements are delayed the more costly it will be to bring the premises up to the standard the public is entitled to expect.

One of the changes made by the Education Reform Act has been to strengthen college governing bodies and to give them the same degree of financial self-management which the schools have attained under the financial delegation sections of the Act. It is the reponsibility of the local authority to give each college board of governors a set of buildings which are sound and serviceable. If, instead, governors inherit substandard premises, many will want at an early date to put in hand a survey of the property for which they are responsible to discover the cost of bringing their premises up to standard.

Having created self-governing colleges, some of which are very large and powerful institutions, the government should now devise an opting-out scheme to allow the larger colleges to become education corporations with full control of their own property. The colleges should then be free to look for ways of managing, and if necessary, redeveloping, parts of their sites to finance improvements and expansion.

There would still need to be capital programmes for specific purposes but if the colleges were allowed to make the most of their assets (and reinvest any capital sums they could realise) it would reward local initiative and secure the best value for money. Colleges are not selling a single product to a single market: they are looking to satisfy many markets with many packages; their premises must be adapted to the diverse demands which students of all kinds make upon them. In the long run, capital costs should be built into the costings of courses and passed on to the various customers the colleges serve.

**Organisation and style**
Every college is different. Each is an organic institution whose development reflects the strengths and weaknesses of the principal, the staff and the governors, as well as the different needs of its industrial and commercial environment. Making governing bodies

stronger and colleges more entrepreneurial will make it even harder to generalise. But it is already becoming clear that new styles will emerge in response to demands.

The Training Agency has pushed hard for change. So too has the National Council for Vocational Qualifications whose initiatives have altered the ground rules within which the colleges operate. And in some cases local authorities have asked fundamental questions about community education and the responsibilities of the colleges to ethnic groups and other underrepresented minorities. The urgency of these questions has been accentuated in some places by the merger of colleges and the creation of large institutions operating out of several separate buildings.

In such circumstances colleges have been prompted to review their activities from scratch, beginning with a new 'mission statement'. Such statements have served as the colleges' publicly adopted formulation of purpose, strategy and values – the basis on which governors, principal and staff intend to operate.

From this some colleges have developed new and more sharply-focused corporate identities and plans, prompting a close examination of their own internal organisation. Such approaches have sometimes been geared to a strengthened college management structure, and a critical review of the departmental organisation with a view to breaking down some of the internal fiefdoms – substituting a reduced number of divisions or 'faculties' for former departmental structures.

The inspiration for the changes which some colleges have introduced has been found in the American community college. There are no exact similes to be drawn because the North American scene is so different from the circumstances on this side of the Atlantic, but one of the things which strikes the English visitor to a Californian community college is its flexibility and the extent which it is geared to the personal needs of its student clients. Colleges are open all hours and at the weekend – whenever, in fact, students can attend. The modular structure of American courses makes for flexibility and for credit accumulation which enables students to continue to study even if they move around or have lengthy breaks in continuity. The colleges take courses to the students at work or in other community buildings. They are proactive – going out to discover what people want, not waiting for them to ask. Many FE colleges have made great strides in the direction of this kind of versatility and it is imperative that more follow them.

The National Council for Vocational Qualifications has also been a powerful influence in encouraging flexibility. Because NVQs are defined strictly in terms of outcomes, with no stipulations about how or where trainees obtain the expertise to meet NVQ competence requirements, some colleges have taken the opportunity to consider alternative ways of providing for student learning. Meeting demand as it surfaces means getting away from rigid entry dates at the beginning of each college year and trying to get something much more like a roll-on, roll-off arrangement.

This, in turn, makes new technology of direct interest and some colleges are adapting parts of their buildings to open access – creating open learning areas where students can learn under the guidance of a tutor, using the available technology of programmed materials and information retrieval.

A feature of the NCVQ approach is the importance attached to the recognition of previous learning, so open learning also needs something like 'assessment on demand', using more electronics to test students before they start and find the base line from which to plan their studies.

FE could well be one of the places where open learning comes into its own most effectively. Progress so far has been sporadic and very uneven. When the Open College was created it was given other educational and commercial objectives: there would have been a great deal to say for using the facilities of a national distance learning organisation to provide a high quality service specially aimed at the colleges. There is still a need for some central support organisation to encourage the spread of open learning in the FE colleges and back it up with specially produced material.

**Work-related**

The colleges will share with private sector organisations, responsibility for meeting the increased demand that will follow if the CBI gets its way. The rate of development will be out of their hands. The volume of the work – the number of student hours – will increase, but it will still be up to the colleges to prove themselves and show they can compete successfully with the other training agencies and in-firm training departments. It will still be up to the colleges to provide attractive conditions of work and attractive teaching packages – attractive both to the students and to the employers.

Much will depend on how the National Council for Vocational Qualifications fares in seeking to extend the range of NVQs which will define the outputs to which the colleges must gear their efforts. If the attempt to build in common skills is successful in a meaningful way, it will give the colleges both an opportunity and a challenge. The colleges still have to defend the fundamental idea of vocational education as a mode of learning which is valid in its own right as a way of individual development. The key to learning may be the inculcation of a specific skill which is of value to an employer and is (in the NCVQ's sense) owned by the employer. But the colleges must aim beyond this in their dealing with young men and women with their lives ahead of them and keep in mind larger educational aims of preparing for uncertainty and continued learning – developing the versatility which goes beyond the immediate to the unknown future. They need to do this, not just to justify their existence as educational institutions, but because the skills revolution, itself, will not take place unless Britain aims high.

How far they are allowed to do this will depend on the employers, the NCVQ and the economic regime which provides the framework for competition which is dealt with in the next chapter. In particular, it is confidently assumed that the TECs will play an important part in influencing the future of FE and of the colleges. Until the role of the TECs becomes clearer, most of the discussion is no more than surmise.

The TECs administer the pilot credit schemes and the large sums of money which lie behind them. It must be assumed that they will want to use the financial power this gives them to influence the colleges and the other training organisations.

**Note**
1. See the various publications from the Further Education Staff College emanating from the MSC-funded Responsive College project.

# Annex: Three colleges

How three colleges have set about adapting to the FE environment is shown in the following pages contributed by college principals.

Newham Community College is a large, diverse, college in East London and Docklands formed when the local authority decided to merge the existing colleges into one large all-purpose FE institution. The principal is John Baillie.

Wirral Metropolitan College is another college formed by merger, which has used the formation of a new institution to think about first principles. The principal is Jenny Shackleton.

Coventry Technical College, one of several Coventry FE colleges, is notable for the way it has entered into the new market-based economy of further education and developed the entrepreneurial skills to flourish under the leadership of the principal, John Temple.

## 1 Newham Community College

*John Baillie writes*:

Since its formation in 1986, Newham Community College has been the single public sector further education organisation in an inner city area which consistently features towards the bottom of the national socio-economic league table. The borough has a 'community education' policy within which the college was, and still is, asked to fulfil three main objectives (themselves a distillation of a fourteen point action programme):

- to ensure that the best educational opportunities are available to all sections of the community;

- to ensure that further education provision within the borough is flexible enough to adapt to the changing needs of the community;

- to ensure maximum benefits from the resources available.

The college engaged in a great deal of proactive marketing activity to determine who our clients are, and what they want. Initial experiments with a centralised marketing unit took us in the wrong direction, provoking territorial disputes and obscuring the need for curriculum groups (a term used in preference to departments) to take full responsibility for marketing.

A devolved marketing structure is now being established whereby the curriculum groups, supported from the centre, identify staff to address the needs of the three broad segments which make up the community – employers, local residents, and schools – and gather information on their needs. Through the college's adequacy and equity projects, a software programme has been developed which can

governors which represents the variety of Newham communities (including its employer members).

The college has consequently developed a great deal of expertise in bidding successfully for a whole range of special grants from a variety of sources – EEC, Education Support Grants, Mutual Development Fund. However, it bids for such grants only when they will take it in the direction it feels it should be going and has used them to develop within the college a range of cross-college posts which have been useful as internal agents of change – embedding in curriculum groups the latest developments in marketing, NVQs, flexible learning, Accreditation of Prior Learning; once these posts have proved their worth the necessary budgetary adjustments are carried out to make them permanent. The proportion of the college budget that comes from income generating courses has been significantly increased – but every care is taken to ensure that benefits from these activities, invested in the form of improved facilities and an enhanced environment, are available to all college users and not just those fortunate enough to be able to pay the full cost of courses.

The college has invested significantly – both in staff and equipment – in computerised management information systems to determine that college services provide value for money in terms of efficiency, effectiveness and equity.

The college is still developing. At the moment, for example, staffing establishments are being restructured to ensure the type of organisation that facilitates the delivery of 'quality education for all'. In sum, the college has spent four years in a process of change predicated upon the belief that no matter how difficult the political and financial climate, a college always has choices.

## 2  Wirral Metropolitan College:  an attempt to become an achievement-led institution.

*Jenny Shackleton writes*:

Wirral Metropolitan College is a large further education college serving the Wirral and its immediate surroundings. In the 1989-90 academic year it enrolled 32,000 (8,200 full-time equivalents), of whom 26,000 were over I8 years of age. It has 600 full-time equivalent lecturers. Its gross budget for the 1990-91 financial year is around £19,000,000. Since 1987 it has been making major and rapid changes to the point where it has acquired a fairly distinctive approach which, for brevity, the college refers to as 'achievement-led institutional development'.

An inspection of the college by HMI in 1986 found it to be sound in many respects, but also lacking both clarity in its purposes and structures, and breadth, diversity and dynamism in its provision and services. The consequences of this were evident in many ways, including declining enrolments and a climate of low expectations and self-esteem.

The published inspection report gave a helpful impetus to an internal review which started in 1987 using the following principles:

- a concern with client groups rather than syllabuses;

- a strategic, long-term approach as a departure from historical roll-forward;

- an external focus instead of internal preoccupations;

- the encouragement of specialisms alongside tolerance of differences;

- corporate-mindedness and mutual support;

- open-mindedness based on full and free information;

- an international perspective in support of local action.

Permeating these principles was the fundamental need for the college to start thinking in purposeful and active ways, by recognising that incisive thought was both a professional obligation and a route to success. Therefore the internal review was thorough and lengthy, in order to develop the understanding and techniques of strategic development and management.

During the two-year period which it took to reorganise, the college grew into an entity which could cope with three tiers of management instead of seven; with many more lateral roles and responsibilities than vertical ones; and with working through teams to tight deadlines.

This emphasis upon staff's individual and collective capability within an overall human resource development strategy mirrors the college's ideals for its students and the local area. These are summed up by the core statements of the college's published mission:

Personal achievement is every individual's right, and the college should organise itself behind this right.

The establishment of personal achievement is a powerful aid to learning and motivation: it should be seen primarily in these terms, within a framework of standards.

The physical, mental and psychological involvement of learners with their own development and achievement, and that of their peers, should be adopted as an organising principle for the college.

Personal achievement should constitute the core mission of the college. To encourage the college to be self-critical about its ability and preparedness to support personal growth, positive appraisal measures should be introduced and developed for learning, teaching and learner support.

The mission with its core of personal achievement was developed following a quite transformational visit to community colleges in the USA by a team of college managers in 1988. The community colleges visited were of similar size to Wirral Metropolitan College; they too served serious community needs. But in other respects the contrasts were staggering for the college team as they traced the implications of a firm commitment to individual achievement through curriculum, organisation, setting and approach. The present character of the college partly reflects the subsequent work done to create similar outcomes to those witnessed, but within a college of further education in the UK at this time.

The first tangible result of the visit was the establishment of an adequate and explicit mission upon which a structure and direction could be based. Education and training is not value-free, and a mature college is one that is capable of working through and articulating its values and purposes. The mission statement is now both the touchstone for, and the perimeter of, the college. The college's strategic planning is based upon it, and decisions taken have to be compatible with it. It is used both corporately and individually.

The logic of an achievement-led approach has forced the college to recognise that an emphasis upon curriculum can inhibit real reform if it concentrates upon lecturers and teaching rather than learners and learning. By regarding learners and learning as distinct issues for attention, the college is now able to consider a wide and radical range of options for maximising learning and achievement among its various client groups. At the present time the college is exploring these in three broad ways.

The first of these is client services. The visit to the USA demonstrated that a lack of client services enforces dependency upon *courses* for both the student and the college, and that it directly inhibits change. Therefore a necessary condition for development at college level was a rapid and major expansion of client services. The diagram (p.64) sets out the services believed to be necessary, and since 1988 the college has been introducing these in a sequence which has been partly logical and partly opportunistic. Short-term external funding has been acquired to help design and monitor a number of the services, such as information and admissions; essentially though, the new client services have come about by the transfer of existing staff resources.

Client services will continue to expand; each new service creates fascinating spin-offs because it enables the clients to relate to the college differently and to contribute in return. A growing number of student-led services are emerging both for the college and the wider community through drama, journalism, other new products and services, and volunteer educational support. Across this range the college is attempting to combine efficiency with creativity, and to avoid undue formality. The new college structure with its college services arm facilitates this,

# A MODEL OF A STUDENT DIRECTED PATHWAY IN F.E.

which illustrates the range of provision and services needed to facilitate it at an institutional level.

LEARNING
INDIVIDUAL
PROGRAMMES
AREAS OF STUDY
COURSES
EDUCATION TRAINING
LIFELONG

INDUSTRY SCHOOL COMMUNITY → STUDENT ENTRY → ADMISSION

| MARKETING | ENQUIRY | PLANNING AND CHOOSING | ENROLMENT | ORIENTATION AND INDUCTION | LEARNING SUPPORT | PERSONAL SUPPORT | WORK EXPERIENCE | ACCREDITATION | EVALUATION | STUDENT EXIT |
|---|---|---|---|---|---|---|---|---|---|---|
| OPEN DAYS WORKSHOPS | STUDENT DATABASE | ASSESSMENT CENTRE | INFORMATION TO STUDENTS | SHORT COURSES | RESOURCES CENTRE | CAREERS ADVICE | WORK PLACEMENTS | SUMMATIVE ASSESSMENTS | STUDENT FEEDBACK | |
| TASTER COURSES | ENQUIRES LOGGED | DIAGNOSTIC INDIVIDUAL ASSESSMENT | FINANCIAL AID | OPEN LEARNING PACKAGES | PERSONAL TUTOR SYSTEM | PERSONAL COUNSELLING | SIMULATED WORK EXPERIENCE | PORTFOLIOS | INPUT INTO COLLEGE REVIEW | |
| ADMISSIONS SEMINARS | STUDENT ADMISSIONS OFFICERS | PRIOR LEARNING ASSESSMENT | STUDENT HANDBOOK | TIME MANAGEMENT STUDY SKILLS LEARNING TO LEARN | FORMATIVE ASSESSMENTS | PEER COUNSELLING | *NROVA | RECORDS OF ACHIEVEMENT | OUTCOMES EXAM RESULTS DESTINATIONS | |
| VISITS CONVENTIONS | | PREFERRED LEARNING STYLES ASSESSMENT | FOLLOW UP EARLY LEAVERS ANALYSIS | BUILDING STUDENT INVOLVEMENT | OPEN LEARNING | *CHILD CARE* FACILITIES | | PRIOR LEARNING ACCREDITATIONS | EXIT & TRANSFER PROGRAMME | |
| REFERALS | | MODE OF ATTENDANCE | *NROVA | | VOLUNTEER PEER TUTORING | HEALTH CENTRES | | *NROVA | | |
| SYSTEMATIC WORD OF MOUTH | | ACTION PLANS | RECORDS OF ACHIEVEMENT | | STUDY CIRCLES | ADULT NETWORK | | CERTIFICATION | | |
| STUDENT NETWORK | | CAREERS GUIDANCE | | | WRITING CENTRES | WOMENS CENTRES | | | | |
| | | | | | | PERSONAL TUTOR | | | | |

* National Record of Vocational Achievement

and client services at present symbolise the tone and relationships by which the college would wish to be characterised in the future.

The college premises provide the second focus for change. The design of most FE colleges is simply unsuitable for the learning and associated activities of the future. The fragmentation and inadequacy of communal areas for reception and client services and for amenities needs addressing, as does the nonsense of having mainly single class size rooms on the one hand, and small offices on the other.

The three main college sites are being remodelled in order to bring together and extend the client services and amenities; to introduce very large versatile spaces for independent study; and to offer initial, formative and summative assessment, and vocational zones with localised back-up, review and transcript services. With thought and imagination major changes can be made for limited cost. However, forward planning and coordination with both client services and curriculum change is vital. Changes in premises are particularly stressful for some staff but liberate many others who have been struggling against their environment. The positive effects at Wirral Met have been most rapidly seen with students and the public in their up-take of services and what they get out of them. In relation to information technology and study support the students can often be more sophisticated than their tutors irrespective of their course content and level.

Thirdly, the college provision in its entirety is now being harmonised. The medium for this is the college 'learning framework' which has been evolved and tested during the last year, and is now being introduced in stages. The framework comprises five elements of harmonisation:

- a categorisation of all provision in terms of core, other elements, and integration;

- the publication of all provision in terms of student learning outcomes;

- the clustering of those outcomes within units of achievement to which is attached credit value;

- the encouragement of Open and Flexible Learning as an alternative or additional learning method to facilitate access and progression;

- and the requirement that all provision has a 'natural pause' at least every 12 weeks, or term, to enable assessment, review and accreditation to be undertaken.

The learning framework builds upon NCVQ's principles; however, it is also designed to be compatible with the existing range of qualifications on offer. Thus it accepts that its outcomes may be criterion-referenced, norm-referenced, or personally-referenced, according to their origins and purposes. Therefore it is a framework for delivery which does not require alternative or additional forms of assessment to those leading to the qualifications now in place; however, it looks forward to a future in which those qualifications merge with a system of transferable units of credit and draws encouragement from NCVQ's broadening remit for core and generic skills, and records of achievement. The framework is activated for staff and students at two levels; the standard programme and individual units, and these are interrelated. The framework is being recorded on DBase 4 software, and will be generally available through the computer network. The learning framework communicates the standards against which people have their prior learning and achievements credited, and it will soon back up on-demand assessment and cumulative accreditation.

These three focuses, client services, premises, and the learning framework, currently provide a structure for the college's forward planning, which endeavours to link over a series of timescales with known and expected policies and trends for further and higher education and training. Inevitably much of this involves second guessing; much also involves taking steps to influence future directions through research and development, networking and demonstration projects; and underpinning this there is a long-term notion of further and higher education characterised by:

- sufficiently-shared curriculum principles to enable articulation between education and training at all levels;

- the joint development of colleges and other providers to offer local networks of learning resources;

- the use of technology and the media in all their forms, as much in relation to education as to training;

- greater autonomy for colleges within a firm and adequate strategic framework;

- measures for client protection and redress.

Without these the ideal of mass participation and achievement is most unlikely to be realised.

### 3 Coventry Technical College – a perspective for the year 2000

*John Temple writes*:

How should the further education colleges develop in the medium term? What will an FE college be like at the beginning of the 21st century? Ideally, it will be:

a) located in the public sector;

b) independent, in that it is governed and managed by people who have a direct interest in its success;

c) entrepreneurial in its culture, behaviour and organisation;

d)  European in that it serves (at least) a European market (as opposed to a local education authority catchment area);

e)  market-led in that its success will be determined by its abilities to sell products in the free and open market;

f)  technology-based in the delivery of learning opportunities.

Its contact with the world outside will be markedly different both in its dealings with clients, consumers and customers, and in its relationships with other colleges. Customers will increasingly demand contractual commitments which may sit uneasily with traditionally accepted obligations to clients and consumers. Other colleges will cease to be nodding acquaintances and become (by economic logic at least) shaking competitors.

There are those who will want to call this a system of FE. The UK has never experienced such: the great strengths and weaknesses of colleges have lain in the fact that no two were exactly similar and that nobody could quite define what their function was. In one sense, this is the chaos of the marketplace; in another, it represents a systematic approach to the provision of vocational education and training including a national infrastructure to underpin our VET industry.

There is an implied contradiction in this argument. Most of the underlying reasoning is based on a recognition of the realities of a free market economy and that organisations in this milieu are best run by leaders and entrepreneurs as opposed to bureaucrats. The obvious question is, why locate this type of college in the public sector at all?

Colleges are selling training and training-related products increasingly on a market basis (strongly encouraged by, for example, the national PICKUP programme and a range of MSC/TA initiatives). I do not believe in any meaningful distinction between 'education' and 'training'. I like the phrase 'Vocational Education and Training'. I believe that strong links with local people and their industrial and business communities represent a logical starting-point for a training institute to operate in a much wider market. This can mean providing some services that would not be viable according to strictly commercial criteria.

There are also the issues of equity, motivation and morale: certain of a college's activities are naturally suited to an entrepreneurial approach. For others this is more difficult: cross-subsidisation within a college can effectively improve morale and performance and secure a wider range of learning opportunities.

A much more important matter is the need to treat VET as a strategic industry in its own right.

Quality training is not an overhead but an important contributor to the bottom line. VET is an industry which supports industry and, if not properly supplied by UK producers, it will increasingly be imported. Key aspects of strategy involve a coherent national (to start with) system of assessment and accreditation which facilitates rather than hinders the integration of alternative learning methods and the application of technology to training. Recent history shows that if colleges themselves do not take the lead in these key national and strategic issues then no one will do it for us.

Colleges need strong leadership and professional management. Civil servants, be they national or local, have not demonstrated a stunning track record of success. Newly constituted boards of governors with independent chairmen and experienced business and industrial leaders are better suited to provide leadership of the new professional cadre of FE managers. LEA catchment areas are an anachronism and, given the new funding arrangements for FE post-ERA, I see no logical or necessary role for LEAs in VET.

Entrepreneurialism, as a 'good thing', has been hammered to death, and is in any case often confused with being business-like.

The most important characteristics of the entrepreneur are the qualities of being outward-looking and risk-taking, and being able to link reward to success. Much of this is alien to the culture of a 'typical' FE college. It is likely to be the 'typical' college which closes, merges or suffers the vicious spiral of decline, reduced funding and more decline. The organisational and reward structures need to support, not hamper, the corporate entrepreneurial goal. But performance-related pay, quasi-autonomous profit centres and a range of types of employment contracts require a different sort of FE manager, and vastly different relationships with trade unions.

European questions have similarly been trivialised by a short-term concern with the single issue of the Single European Market of 1992.

We are into something much bigger: a belief in a common Europe (which is a great deal wider than the existing EC states) and a commitment to pan-European training systems in an increasingly integrated European economy. This is much more fundamental than teaching of language skills and the exchange of staff and students. We urgently need to develop common competence-based training programmes which are European rather than multi-national in character. We do not see it as a question of exporting into Europe – more a statement of the irrelevance, in itself, of which country one is producing in. Concrete examples of this approach are the establishment of a joint venture Coventry Technical College in Athens, and the establishment of a college office in Brussels to act as the hub of a European FE network.

Being market-led is more fundamental than responding to business needs. Colleges need to understand that, whether they like it or not, the funding arrangements of delegated budgets, training subsidies being passed to TECs, and the emergence of a system of training credits, redistributes subsidy from the supplier (the colleges) to the customer (most likely industry or commerce) and the consumer (the student).

Colleges are rapidly losing their privileged position vis à vis the private sector provider: the best colleges will not be afraid to take on the private sector on its own terms and win. We need to sell on the basis of quality (in the sense of guaranteed training outcomes) rather than price alone. Fee per successful student is a logical concomitant of unit cost per successful student, and we anticipate increasing numbers of contracts with industry based on successful outcomes.

Technology is central to the effective and efficient delivery of training. Classroom teaching is but one example of available learning techniques. Colleges which adopt the best practices of distance and open learning based on the best technology-based training products will have a remarkable competitive edge. Higher quality at lower cost will be accompanied by the ability to deliver training anywhere in Europe. But there is, of course, a price; heavy initial investment is needed to enter this virtuous circle and this investment is not forthcoming from traditional sources. It is being made from income earned from colleges themselves, but even that is not enough. Central questions of competencies, accreditation and qualification transfers are still dealt with in splendid isolation.

I am sure that my college will survive and prosper into the 21st century. We have a corporate strategy that almost guarantees this. Perhaps not every college can emulate this success, but it is a necessary, albeit insufficient, condition for a prosperous UK VET System that most try. The complacent would do well to remember that FE has no natural constituency of support and the gradual demise of public sector FE is not impossible. Optimistic realists need to band together. The success of the best colleges needs to be synergised to force the strategic restructuring of VET in the UK and in Europe.

# 4  Finance and Organisation

Serving multiple aims and diverse clients, further education necessarily requires more than one paymaster. It would make matters a lot easier if FE could be assigned a single function, for example, vocational education, and told to get on with it. But this is not possible – the messiness and confusion is part of what further education is all about.

The Education Reform Act reflects this. Section 120 spells out the extensive nature of the FE commitment; it imposes on every local education authority the duty to 'secure the provision for their area of adequate facilities for further education' and defines FE as 'full- or part-time education for persons over compulsory school age (including vocational, social, physical and recreational training)' and related leisure-time activities.

From the definition it follows that there are liable to be sharp political questions about local as well as national priorities in further education. FE is a local community resource. It exists to meet the needs of the local community and the local labour market as well as perceived national requirements. Some of these local needs are easily aligned with current national policy – as for example in the priority attached to vocational education and training, both for the 16 to 19s and for adults of all ages. There are other areas of activity which may throw up differences of emphasis and priority between the local authority and central government. The concept of the community college, with its well-articulated obligations to all sections of the community, including minorities and hitherto underrepresented groups, draws heavily on local politics and pressure groups.

FE's traditional functions as the provider of second chances have been developed within a paternalist philosophy of municipal public service and funding. The current national priorities are about vocational education and training and are geared to industry's need to close the skills gap which overrides all other needs – or would do, were it feasible to ignore all other community concerns. In reality many of these community concerns are highly relevant to vocational education in that for many adults, basic 'second chance' education and English language skills are a prerequisite for future employment and learning. In considering how far different functions should be paid for from different pockets, it is important to recognise that across a wide range of further education, the separate programmes are complementary, not competing.

## Further education college funding

In recent years college funding has come from three main sources. First, *the local education authorities* who, in accordance with their statutory duty, are the main financial supporters of the further education colleges. Taking the colleges as a whole, about 80 per cent of their budgets are met by local authority funding.

The Act applies the same principles of financial delegation and local management to FE as to schools. Local education authorities must prepare a scheme for funding in accordance with Section 139 of the 1988 Act. This must be submitted to the Secretary of State for his approval. Each college gets its 'budget share' of what the local authority decides to spend on FE, calculated under a weighted per capita formula based on the number of full-time equivalent students and the mix of subjects. The first draft of the plan is worked up by the local authority from bids from its colleges which reflect their estimates of local demand.

This 'scheme' is the basis of the local authority's planning function. Legally, the authorities have formidable powers to decide between the competing claims of the colleges and to lay down their own distinctive policies. In practice these powers are limited: they have up till now been shared with the Training Agency which, in principle, has controlled a quarter of the spending on work-related further education (WRFE) and indirectly influenced the rest. Under the Education Reform Act, the planning role of the Department of Education and Science will become more important because the Education Secretary's approval is required for every scheme. There remains the potential for tension between the DES and the Department of Employment, which is assuming some of the residual activities of the TA.

Secondly, FE colleges have received funding from *some government departments and from the European Commission.* They have received money from the Department of Employment under provisions for Youth Training and Employment Training and other programmes. About 10-11 per cent of expenditure is covered from these agency fees. From 1992, these will come within the purview of the Training and Enterprise Councils. There have also been various project funds distributed by the Training Agency. These have included the Mutual Development Fund taken from the WRFE money under TA control. The active research and development pursued by the TA and the seed money distributed under programmes run by the Department of Trade and Industry have provided useful sources on which colleges have been able to draw. So too for some colleges have grants from the European Social Fund and other parts of the European Community. The sums involved have seldom been large but have been significant within the economy of some colleges.

The third source of funding includes *fees of all kinds paid by students and by companies for training contracts.* In principle, individual students under 18 pay no fees and some LEAs waive fees for some other categories (such as unemployed adults). The colleges receive a contribution towards the cost of under-18s on YTS which seems to breach this principle (the subject of acrimonious wrangling between the local authority associations and the MSC in the past), but college provision – for, say, day release courses for apprentice electricians or full-time A level students – would normally be provided out of the college's share of the local authority budget.

Generally speaking, students aged 19 and over have to pay fees. College fees have in the past been heavily subsidised. In recent years, the levels of subsidy have been reduced, particularly in many forms of adult education and recreational provision, and fees now represent a useful element in college funding (of the order of 10 per cent).

Colleges have been encouraged to develop services for employers wanting specialised courses for the up-dating of skills through schemes such as the DES's PICKUP. Some colleges have been very successful in selling 'customised' training packages to employers who are prepared to pay the full cost (and an element of profit) for well-designed schemes of high quality. These will include some courses on employers' premises and some consultancy services. How successful colleges are in generating income by this sort of activity depends largely on local circumstances and the degree of enthusiasm with which they have approached the task. Some have been markedly more energetic than others.

Coventry Technical College (see page 66) is the outstanding example of a college which has sought to expand this side of its activities.

According to its most recent (1989) annual report, its total budget amounted to £9,650,000, of which only £5,958,000 (62 per cent) came from the local education authority. Some £2,123,000 was raised by services which were charged out at full cost.

## Changes in the pipeline

Changes in the background circumstances introduce a number of new factors. While the colleges' new governing bodies settle down and find their feet, the local authorities are coming to terms with the community charge. Capping and the threat of capping constrain budgets while at the same time there are calls for more, not less activity.

More uncertainty is introduced by the demise of the Training Agency and the arrival (at an uneven pace) of TECs, the scope of whose activities remains to be established. Moreover, the government has acted quickly to pick up the CBI's proposals for training credits, with eleven pilot schemes, starting in 1991. Ten schemes will be administered by TECs in England and Wales, one by Grampian Local Enterprise Council in Scotland. The cumulative effect of all these changes leaves further education in a state of wary expectation. The signals are coming in thick and fast. Not all of them are consistent.

Two patterns of finance and organisation can be discerned as possible scenarios for a future in which vocational education and training expand in line with the CBI proposals.

The first of these may be called the status quo in transition; the second, the market model:

### *The status quo in transition*

Funding would continue to come from a mixture of sources with the local authority providing the biggest share. This would, as now, reflect the diverse range of services which are provided and the convenience of having an administrative structure based on the major units of local government.

Further education for the under-19s remains an entitlement without fee and rather than seek to make the employers pay more of the cost of the services provided for them by the colleges for these students, the state would signal its commitment to the expansion of vocational education and training by underwriting increased expenditure through the Revenue Support Grant.

The other sources of college income remain unchanged, except that TECs take over responsibility for most of what has hitherto been done by the Training Agency. The expectation would be that the TECs are more active in defining local industrial and commercial priorities than the Training Agency has been hitherto. This would mean looking again at the 25 per cent of work-related further education funding which has till now been (in theory) under the control of the Training Agency. As this passes to the TECs they will have the financial muscle to intervene strongly in local FE budget-making and, if they wish to, to play off one authority against another in search of the best value for the money at their disposal.

Local authorities will continue to have some responsibility for quality and for staff development. Control of curriculum will rest with the colleges themselves and the examining bodies which their students must satisfy. But the long-stop responsibilities of the local education authority will certainly extend to making sure that the quality of education – and quality of life – offered by colleges to students is not sacrificed when colleges position themselves for the aggressive marketing of full-cost services to industry and commerce.

The pressure on the colleges to market their services will build up as it becomes clear that some colleges are very much more successful in augmenting their income by selling training and consultancy packages than others. As with the universities and colleges, a premium will be put on these entrepreneurial activities and no college will be able to flourish which does not raise a substantial part of its income in this way.

*Planning considerations*
The DES clearly regards the local authority's planning function as very important. A prime aim is to ensure that courses are economically distributed. This is reflected in the legislation which emphasises the need to consult all the relevant institutions – colleges and schools, public and private – in drawing up the local scheme. Avoiding overlap and duplication has been a traditional concern of successive

governments in the management of further education. There always has to be a trade-off between the needs of local employers and the need to share provision economically among the colleges. This will continue, but the influence of the employers will increase as TECs become effective.

While the local authorities' planning functions remain central to the arrangements for the allocation of the main funding, other developments point less towards rational planning than the release of market forces to which colleges will be expected to respond. Competition and choice – concepts which are fundamental to the Education Reform Act – are to be much more important.

If, as we have seen, a college is to market its strengths and those services which bring the best return, this may well conflict with the plans of local authorities. College governors, not local authorities, will control the revenues earned by entrepreneurial activities. At this stage of their development they may be willing to use the profits from their more lucrative private sector contracts to subsidise other, unprofitable but worthy, college activities favoured by the local authority. But such cross-subsidisation is at odds with the logic of a competitive system offering the best services to customers at the lowest cost – the customers with most muscle being employers.

It must be fairly obvious that it is going to be very difficult to constrain a college like Coventry within the limits of a local authority plan if it comes to a struggle of wills and the LEA is bearing a diminishing share of the cost. And if the motive in seeking to curb the activities of one college is to protect courses in some other neighbouring college which is less efficient (and less attractive to students and employers) it will be even harder to justify. Moreover, the ambitions of some boards of governors may well stretch beyond the immediate environs of the college – they may be drawing students and business from farther afield. Some colleges emphasise the importance of the European dimension in training and intend to go after business throughout the European Community. Whatever the merits of such developments, they promise to make local authority planning increasingly difficult.

The introduction of the pilot scheme for training credits is another added complication. Planning becomes even more problematical if training credits are to be used to channel any substantial part of the finance for FE through trainees' vouchers instead of the colleges' share of local authority funds. The theoretical aim of a voucher scheme is to give the power of decision to the consumer and take it away from the provider. So long as the scheme remains experimental no great difficulty arises: we shall return to the wider considerations later.

The increased autonomy which the Act gives college governors does not remove the local authority's ultimate responsibility. If it came to a crunch, the Act makes it perfectly clear that the LEA, backed by the Secretary of State, could force a college to toe the line. But that is not the point – the point is that there is a conflict between the traditional DES wish for a system of predictable size and cost in which local colleges are restrained or prodded to fulfil their prescribed part, and the market model (to which the DES is also now committed). The former reflects the tradition of public sector education over a century and more: the latter gives expression to the philosophy of the Education Reform Act. The modified status quo does not look strong enough to withstand the stresses which would be set up by this conflict over any length of time.

### The market model
Under the second scenario, there would continue to be funding from a variety of sources. These would include the same main sources of finance but the balance would be different.

### Credits or vouchers
The present scheme of training credits would be extended stage by stage to cover more and more of the users of further education. The first move would be for the 11 pilot schemes to be enlarged to take in the whole country and all school-leavers.

According to Michael Howard, the Secretary of State for Employment, announcing the launch of the pilots on August 30, 1990:

> the objectives of each scheme are to increase the motivation of young people to continue with quality training and vocational education when they join the labour market, as well as to increase the numbers of young people in training and the levels of their qualifications.[1]

Credits (like education vouchers) are seen as a powerful way of increasing competition within the education and training system and releasing market forces as a stimulant to efficiency and responsiveness. They will cover specified costs of education and training provided by FE colleges and private sector training organisations. As well as showing the trainee that his or her training has a cash value, credits will create an incentive for colleges to make their services attractive to 'credit-holders', thereby increasing the competition between colleges, and between colleges and private sector training agencies. This will also force colleges to make a proper business plan, analyse their costs and be clear about how they are distributed between various college activities. Because they will be more dependent on market forces, colleges will have to study the needs of their industrial customers more closely; success or failure will depend on how well this is done.

For those who leave school at 16 and enter employment, the voucher would be a two-year entitlement to take to an employer and in an ideal world the young would-be employee would contract his labour to the employer who made the best training offer. The short-term demographic trend is likely to strengthen the hands of the teenagers in the market place: credits could conceivably be an incentive for teenagers to use their scarcity value to demand better training rather than more money. It will certainly encourage recruiters to advertise what they intend to do about training.

But it is not realistic to suppose that the voucher will place much power in the hands of the newest recruit. The training credit is unlikely to affect most young people's job choice or the eclectic range of people and events which influence it. Credits could still be important, however, if they contributed in a small but public way to the change in attitudes which are demanded by the skills revolution. It is necessary always to remember that what is needed is nothing less than a profound change in the culture. Credits should be seen, in part at least, as a way of telling everyone that a new dispensation is at hand. No-one, however, should underestimate the complexity of a credit scheme extended across the board: the idea is attractive, but only if it can be made to work in practice. As for the government's pilot credit scheme, it is also important as a first step by the government towards accepting the CBI argument that public money should cover the cost of the education and training for foundation skills, leaving employers to pay the trainees' wages, where appropriate. As has been indicated, the CBI position is logical and ought to be accepted unequivocally. At the same time, the government should assert its right to take a view on where the public interest lies in training and monitor what happens in private sector training organisations as well as in the colleges.

*16 to 19: full and part-time* If a credit scheme is a good idea for those who leave school and enter employment with part-time vocational education and training, it ought to be beneficial as a way of dealing with the funding of those in full-time education as well. At an early stage the scheme should be extended to all 16 to 19s so that credits are available to cover the cost of full-time education in school or FE college as well as part-time education and training in public or private institutions. This would be a natural corollary to the aim of planning the years 14 to 18 as a whole and reducing the significance of the break at 16: it is important to motivate the stayers-on as well as those who take the part-time route to vocational qualifications.

If all education and training for the 16-19 age groups is brought within the framework of a credit scheme, some interesting possibilities arise. It has been stressed that credits are to be valid for training in private sector training agencies as well as in further education colleges. If they are to be extended across the board, the question is: should they be available for all approved forms of education – schools as well as FE colleges; private sector institutions as well as those run by local education authorities? Should people be allowed to use them to pay the fees at independent schools?

There is a powerful logic which says that they should. True, there would be some 'dead-weight' spending as a result – some people who would otherwise pay fees out of their own pockets would become eligible for credits. But there would be enormous advantages in opening up the sixth forms of the independent schools to all comers – or at least, to more comers.

The obvious analogy would be with the opening up of the universities after the second world war. In the post-war world, access to the universities was widened by the simple device of paying the fees of all acceptable candidates. So, today, any student who can win a place in a university or other institution of higher education receives the equivalent of a training credit from his or her local authority. The government of the day might have considered only the question of the 'dead-weight' – the fees which were already being paid under the old arrangements. Or they might have devised a training credit which could only be used at the public sector colleges of the time, thereby limiting and distorting choice and restricting competition. Instead it was decided to treat public and private sector institutions alike and open them all to qualified entrants. To pursue this analogy might raise the question of whether it was wise to abolish fees to students – a question made the more relevant by the devious attempts of ministers and some vice-chancellors to reintroduce them now. But whether it was wise or unwise to abolish fees, it was certainly right to treat public and private sector institutions in the same manner and mobilise them all for the nation. The same strategy should apply in the case of the independent schools because they constitute a great national resource and provide a quarter of all available post-16 places in secondary schools.

It has to be conceded that this raises as many questions as it answers: what is to be the value of the credit or voucher? The training credits cover services of varying value with the same voucher but the providers will have to be paid for what they provide on agreed terms. There would be a strong case for limiting the dead-weight costs by making credits cashed at independent schools subject to a steep means test (like assisted school places).

Of course, any such scheme would be politically fraught. It would certainly be attacked by those who see any attempt to integrate public and private education as a reinforcement of privilege. But the credit itself is value-free: the small print could weight a scheme with any chosen set of social or economic values. It would, for example, be quite possible, given current priorities, to build in incentives for those who choose the vocational route.

*Adults* Having extended credits to the whole of the 16-19 cohort in the first phase, it would be time to move on to the second phase and introduce credits selectively for other FE users as part of the build up of skill training envisaged in the CBI proposals. This would reinforce incentives to the colleges to tailor their activities to the needs of employers and adult students, some of whom would be bearing all or part of the cost themselves.

All in employment should qualify for credits up to a certain value without any restriction on when they could use them: adult credits would not necessarily cover the whole of the fee for any particular course – it would still be in order to expect the students, themselves, or their employers to pay some of the cost.

A credit card for every individual as a mechanism for distributing purchasing power in further and adult education is an exciting idea and could offer a powerful and flexible tool for achieving a learning society. One such idea is explored in the report from Employment UK following a consultation held at St George's House, Windsor, in the spring of 1990.[2]

It should be possible for employees to build up funds to meet their part of the cost through an employer-subsidised insurance scheme. It might be thought desirable to create some priority categories – for example, married women returning to the labour force after a period away might qualify for a credit towards retraining; so might men and women made redundant or those willing to retrain to acquire skills which are in short supply.

Again, one of the main aims would be psychological – to create the idea of an entitlement as well as a prudent awareness of the benefits accruing to continued training. And there would be justice in allowing those who had left school early to receive (in the form of a credit) some of the money they had already saved the public purse.

The merit of any scheme would depend, however, not on the principle but on the detail and any plan would inevitably have to be extremely complicated if it were to cover a wide range of possibilities and circumstances. If a scheme were too complicated there would be a risk that it would become submerged in the bureaucratic regulations which the simplicity of a 'smart' card was intended to sidestep.[2]

*Management* As managers of the credit schemes it would fall to the Training and Enterprise Councils to decide on the priorities and the speed at which these schemes should be extended, having regard to their financial situation and the cash limits placed upon their activities.

It has already been suggested that the provision of training credits for school-leavers implies an acceptance on the part of the government that the costs of vocational education and training, up to the age of 19, in FE and in private sector organisations, should be met from public funds – an acceptance which the government has been coy about spelling out in terms. The financial arrangements for the TECs make it necessary to remove any remaining doubt about the division of financial responsibility. In taking over Youth Training and Employment Training, the TECs open their accounts with large sums of government money. But the major part of the Youth Training money goes on the provision of training opportunities for young people who might otherwise be unemployed – the Youth Training Scheme never managed to shed its origins in the improvised anti-youth unemployment measures of the early 1980s. It was seen by many young people and employers as a palliative exercise – an attempt to make good an employment deficit. Likewise, Employment Training emerged as a controversial attempt to get the long-term unemployed off the unemployment register. True, Youth Training also helps to fund what remains of craft training after the collapse of apprenticeship but, leaving this aside, the TECs are likely to see their responsibilities for these two programmes as performing a service to the government rather than doing something which directly meets their own vocational education and training needs and makes industry more profitable.

Cuts in the funding of the programmes that are being turned over to the TECs have done nothing to dim the impression that the employers and the politicians are interpreting the rhetoric in different ways. The sooner the assumptions that underlie the credit scheme are extended to other parts of the vocational education and training scene, the better for all concerned.

Within the market culture which a credit scheme implies, there would certainly have to be quality controls – agreed standards which any organisation providing services in return for credits would have to meet.

It is a complaint among employers that the present FE system offers little 'transparency' in the matter of standards. How are they to know whether they are getting value for money?

One possible answer may be found in the readiness of the most entrepreneurial colleges to talk of using output measures – that is, asking the employer to pay fees only for students who pass the assessment or examination at the end of the course. This could certainly be seen as a logical extension of the NCVQ approach – albeit one which most colleges would feel threatened by. What is beyond doubt is that the decision to entrust the rationalisation of vocational qualifications to the NCVQ has been taken and its competence-based model of assessment is the model that is going to prevail. Other methods of monitoring the quality of the educational process in colleges of further education exist but the ultimate measure is going to be the success or failure of trainees as measured by NVQs.

Such an approach must leave unanswered questions about the quality of the experience which a college offers. It is quite easy to imagine two colleges which achieve identical results in terms of NVQs, but one of which can be immediately recognised as 'better' than the other. Throughout the system – at the LEA level, in each college, and in Her Majesty's Inspectorate – there must be a passionate concern about quality which goes beyond the crude statistics of NVQs gained. An interesting development of recent years has been the interest of the British Standards Institute. The ultimate performance indicators have yet to be found but the search should go on.

The logic of the CBI proposals would be to regard vocational education and training for the adult working population as a demand-led requirement to be expanded as fast as practically possible. And as industry will be expected to meet most of the cost there is no reason why development should not go ahead as fast as the employers are prepared to move. It remains to be seen whether the CBI initiative will generate the necessary momentum among employers to lead to rapid development, and what happens when there is a down-turn in business activity as in the winter of 1990-91. This must, of course, be a matter of considerable interest to the colleges: the more entrepreneurial they become, the more vulnerable they will be to market conditions.

### Local education authorities

If further education for the 16 to 19 year-olds is funded by credits, and if the costs of an increasing proportion of adult work are also met by credits and fees and full-cost contracts, there would be a corresponding reduction of the share of FE funding borne by local education authorities through the Revenue Support Grant and the community charge.

The local education authority's role would be concentrated on other aspects of FE such as special needs, adult education, community education and Access programmes. These, too, could be promoted by the use of credits to increase public awareness and to emphasise the right of credit-holders to choose where to go to find the courses or services which best meet their needs. This would tie up with the idea of education credit cards for adult retraining – local authorities could contribute, on their own terms, to the credit which individuals might build up over time. This would not be in any way inconsistent with the adoption by the local authority of its own community priorities. Behind the idea, however, is the correct assumption that the more successful the attempt to put Britain's education and training house in order, the more obvious the need for more adult education will become and the greater the disadvantage of those who get left behind.

The effect of the changes aimed at making vocational education more directly related to the needs of employers and individuals must be to leave the ostensibly non-vocational aspects of further education in an exposed position. It would become harder to cross-subsidise these activities from other FE revenues. He would be a brave man who was confident that enough money would be provided to maintain the full range of further education services set out in the Act. But it would bring the value questions out into the open and force politicians and public to confront them and debate their impact on the quality of life. What would be very unsatisfactory would be for local debate on these matters – which will be materially influenced by the local environment and mix of community needs and interests – to be foreclosed by a system of local government finance which left little room for local manoeuvre – as for instance where local taxing powers are, in effect, suspended by poll-tax capping.

## Other sources

There would probably still need to be some residual funding by the Department of Employment but the logic would be to end the flow of new programmes and give the TECs their head. But this has to be recognised as a high risk strategy which banks on the capacity of the TECs to achieve something like coherence. It seems most unlikely that any government could carry this hands-off approach through to its logical conclusion – even if that were thought to be desirable – and there will continue to be a need for the latter-day equivalent of the Training Agency to prod and pump-prime.

## Planning

A market model, by definition largely eliminates the local authority planning function. Colleges compete; successful colleges thrive; unsuccessful colleges go to the wall. There is no concern about the waste that follows from competitive duplication: it is more than compensated for by the increased efficiency which competitive enterprise will bring.

In practice, that may not be how it works out, but the limitations on the LEA planning role will be real enough. The local authority will still have to make plans for its continuing FE responsibilities but these will not cover the priority business of the colleges in vocational education and training. The colleges will have to respond to the short-term wants of the credit-holders and the employers who effectively control their financial destiny. In particular they will have to satisfy the TECs who, if the government puts them in funds, will be

83

in a strong position to implement their separate plans – always provided they know what they want and that what they want coincides with the wants expressed by individual employers and credit-holders.

Capital development would depend on the prosperity of each college. The cost of borrowing would have to be built into the fees charged and the credits accepted. This would enhance the autonomy of the colleges but carry with it the risk – the certainty – that development would be uneven. But does this matter? The true marketeers would claim that it is much more important to build up strong colleges than to achieve a well-managed mediocrity.

Within the British tradition, an FE college is small beer and the natural inclination of administrators will be to keep it that way. But must this necessarily be so? Why should not some colleges excel – develop national reputations, as some schools do? It is only necessary to visit a few of the leading community and junior colleges in the United States to recognise that colleges which are mainly dealing with non-advanced work can nevertheless be powerful institutions, capable of setting and maintaining their own high standards and managing their own destinies.

### The market metaphor
At the heart of the question of planning is the nature of the market for vocational education and training. Is there a real market or only a simulation of a market? Market metaphors are powerful, but they are still metaphors. Credits are to be provided by government to replace money hitherto paid directly to local authorities and training organisations: they are to create the likeness of a market, but one which is artificial – one which is to be managed – rigged – to provide the outcomes which the government wants. Public money still has to be laid out because the real market (in which employers spend most of their time) does not by itself sustain training on the scale required. This is the truth about the training market which must never be obscured by ideology or rhetoric.

### National strategy
The inference must be that there will still be a need for national strategic planning and for national monitoring to see how the interests of the nation are being served in return for the large sums of public money with which this market is being lubricated. The leading role

attributed to industry and commerce does not detract from this ultimate responsibility of government. Nor does it mean that the colleges, themselves, can play a proper part in the planning process without a strong national organisation to match the collective organisations which will speak for industry and the TECs.

There should be, then, first, a combined Department of Education and Training with a clear remit to set national targets for both vocational education and training and to make sure they are being achieved – to attend to those tasks which the short-term imperatives of the market cannot in the nature of things deal with. Someone has to take responsibility for the infrastructure and make sure that there are enough trained teachers and trainers. Because, at the end of the day, there are national interests at stake, and because the individual is entitled to some external assurances about quality, a strong inspectorate is needed combining (and improving upon) functions hitherto carried out by the DES and the Department of Employment's Training Agency.

Secondly, the colleges should build up a strong central organisation which can represent them in national negotiations and lobby government and industry on their behalf.

The analogy is with the associations representing the community and junior colleges in the United States and the formidable clout mustered by the organisations which share an office block at Washington's Dupont Circle. The Association of Colleges for Further and Higher Education was not created to fulfil this role – indeed as Geoffrey Melling, the director of the Further Education Staff College, has argued forcefully, the role is only now being created by current developments.[3] Such a body must be financed by the colleges, out of their revenues – 400 colleges with revenues of the order of £1 billion clearly have the resources to set up such an association if they wish to do so. Till now decisions on such matters have been in the hands of the local authorities, who, like the government, have no particular wish to see a strong and independent voice for the colleges. Future decisions will be for college governors. They should start at once to think about the kind of organisation they need, and how and over what period it could be built up. Each college will be a semi-autonomous, competitive, unit but they will still need to club together nationally to punch their collective weight.

**Notes**
1. The programme of pilot projects was announced in parliament on 27 March 1990 and details of the selected areas were given at a press conference by Michael Howard, Secretary of State for Employment, and Tim Eggar, Minister of State at the Department of Education and Science on 30 August 1990.
2. See Full Employment UK, *Investing in Skills – Part Three*, a report of the third in a series of consultations at St George's House, Windsor, 1990.
3. Geoffrey Melling, Director of the Further Education Staff College, 'Collective Management: the Critical Issues', address to the Summer Meeting of the Association of Colleges for Further and Higher Education, June 1989.

# 5  Conclusion

1.  The first conclusion is basic.  It is this.  There exists a strong consensus about:
*   the need to achieve a longer period of initial education for more people;
*   the need to ensure, as the CBI and the TUC propose, that all young people continue till at least 18 in full-or part-time education and/or training, leading to a recognised qualification.

As a nation, we must now so arrange our affairs as to make these things happen. This is the first necessity.

The consensus breaks down about whether the CBI's aims can be realised without a statutory framework. The Labour Party believes that a statutory framework will be needed to bring about the changes that the CBI and the TUC want to see. The Conservatives, on the other hand, accept the view of the industrialists that the results can be attained by voluntary means.

What the Conservative Government should now do is accept the CBI proposals in principle as national policy, adopt targets for implementation and undertake to monitor progress.

If, under the leadership of the Training and Enterprise Councils, things go ahead fast, well and good. If things move ahead smoothly, well and good. If not, the government must stand committed to doing what is necessary to maintain the momentum of development.

It follows from this that the government must look closely at the economics of training. The total commitment of employers is essential if the ultimate aim of a world-class workforce for a high productivity, high pay, economy is to be achieved. The orthodox view that training is first and foremost the responsibility of industry and commerce reflects this reality. But the corollary to this is that the government must create a financial regime which provides the incentive for employers to train.

It is clear that in simple, short-term, balance sheet terms, employers find it cheaper to poach trained staff from other companies or to import components (and export jobs) rather than set up the kind of expensive training operations which their competitors in, say, Germany maintain. If training is to remain the responsibility of industry and the market, the government cannot evade its obligation to rig that market to make training worth industry's while, in good times and in bad. Experience has shown that shareholders will not shoulder the costs by themselves.

2. The second basic conclusion is that Britain – and especially England – is under-educated as well as under-trained. Too many boys and girls drop out of education at the earliest opportunity. This gives particular importance to what the CBI calls the foundation stage. This is not, of course, the only stage: the demands of older age-groups must also be met. But it makes good sense to begin by trying to create a better foundation on which all future efforts can be based.

One reason for the under-education of the English is the failure to find a way of integrating general and vocational education. This is as true now as it was in the last quarter of the 19th century when it was institutionalised in government in the separate activities of the Science and Art Department (part of the Board of Trade) and the Education Department. Such a division still persists in the separate activities of the Department of Employment and the Department of Education and Science. For much of the 1980s the tension between the two departments produced more debilitating friction than creative tension.

We need therefore:

- a single Department of Education and Training;
- and, without waiting for a change in the machinery of government, a review of the curriculum offered to boys and girls between the ages of 14 and 18 – partly in schools, partly in colleges of further education – full- and part-time.

3. The aim should be to map out clear paths for all in the relevant age-groups, spanning the school-leaving age. For some, this will mean a well-defined set of options flagged by the various examinations for general and vocational education. For others it will mean a mixture of the general and the vocational. For others, again, it will lead through

entry into employment into vocational education and training on a part-time basis, leading to recognised qualifications (NVQs).

4. School examinations come under the School Examinations and Assessment Council. Vocational qualifications are the responsibility of the National Council for Vocational Qualifications. In sorting out the educational provision for the 14 to 18s, they need to come together with the specific aim of providing a complementary set of options. A joint council should be formed from the National Curriculum Council, the School Examinations and Assessment Council, the National Council for Vocational Qualifications and the Further Education Unit, charged with the task.

In this it will be important to strengthen the vocational options and weave them more effectively into the mainstream of educational opportunity. In this the colleges of further education have an essential part to play. Vocational education already exists as an alternative route. The initial aim must be to mark this route more clearly, and to create the guidance and counselling services needed to help young people take good decisions about their future. The longer-term aim must be to create, not an alternative system, but one which is complementary. This implies the continued development of modular curricula to blur the edges between general and vocational education.

5. With this must go improved guidance and counselling to help all students to negotiate action plans to which they and their schools or colleges would be committed. Such plans should be incorporated into on-going records of achievement.

6. Critical consideration will have to be given to the role of the National Council for Vocational Qualifications in regard to this process of rationalisation. In particular, there is the question of the role of the Industry Lead Bodies and how, and how far, their influence should be brought to bear on the content of vocational courses (and examinations) for those who remain in full-time education up to 18. The NCVQ has established methods of working that concentrate wholly on outcomes, ignoring the process by which students and trainees reach the levels of competence that are demanded. To provide a robust framework for an expanded education system, it will be necessary to take a close interest in process as well, to provide a breadth of experience as well as specific skills.

7. The Business and Technician Education Council is well placed to play a central role in any attempt to strengthen the vocational route,

having a well-established system of diplomas and certificates which provide for full- and part-time students.

8. As for the colleges of further education, they constitute a great and under-used resource. Most people live within reasonable travelling distance of a college. They are adaptable and have a tradition of service to local industry and to community needs. There is a need to build on the work done in the past decade that has shown how colleges can be made more flexible, open and responsive to the needs of students of all ages.

9. Developments in information technology and independent learning need to be fostered, together with the provision of customised services for industry and commerce. The Training and Enterprise Councils' influence will increase the pressure on colleges to respond entrepreneurially to the needs of industry – needs which will grow rapidly if the CBI targets are achieved. The colleges will be in competition with private sector training organisations. There is ample room for both of them.

10. Other community needs must also be covered if the further education system is to meet the requirements of the Education Reform Act. In the present context, the leverage to action is provided by the awareness that Britain must achieve the 'skills revolution' required to make British industry more competitive. This makes vocational education the obvious focus. Much of what takes place in colleges under the banner of community education is also of direct or indirect vocational relevance – as, for example, in providing basic education for non-English speakers or special courses for people trying to get back into employment.

11. This makes it important to maintain a diversity of funding for further education. The local education authority has funding and planning functions which appear to be in conflict with the market philosophy on which the TECs have been founded. The experiment with training credits suggests that more of the money for further education will come to the colleges from a source other than the LEA, and in a manner designed to encourage competitive entrepreneurship on the part of college principals. If this happens, it will be necessary to look again at the local authority planning function.

12. To compete successfully, college buildings need to be brought up to standard, and they must be able to undertake the minor works required to respond quickly to changing demands. If the colleges are to be seen as lively and popular places, they must be enabled to present

themselves in attractive and welcoming circumstances. The more they are expected to sell their services to business, the more important these considerations become. In the past there has been a deplorable willingness to neglect the maintenance of educational buildings of all kinds. If this continues the contribution of the colleges will be diminished.

13. Training credits are an imaginative way of raising consciousness about training and focussing the attention of employers and new entrants on the training dimension., If the pilot schemes justify their extension to all young school-leavers – and eventually to all the 16-19s – they would have far-reaching consequences, some of which have been explored in Chapter 4. As a means of funding what the CBI calls 'careership', credits could provide a subtle and flexible way of channelling money into personal and vocational development – with contributions from the employer, the individual, the Inland Revenue and (as appropriate, for priority groups) from central and local government.

# Index